"With his latest book, *Remaining Relev* the ultimate success blueprint for ε Accounting firm. His global knowl what does not is unmatched. He has hit the nail on the head with how Accountants will be disrupted by technology. This is the start of the end of professional services as we know it."

Verne Harnish, CEO Gazelles, Founder of Entrepreneurs
Organization, and author of 'Scaling Up (Rockefeller Habits 2.0)',
'The Greatest Business Decisions of All Time', and
'Mastering the Rockefeller Habits'
Ashburn, Virginia, USA

"Throughout my career I've had the opportunity to work with inspiring people who are hugely passionate about what they do. Buoyant people with boundless energy who have a willingness to share their passion and knowledge, imparting the lessons they have learned and the experiences that have had. Tenacious people who never give up… ever. Rob Nixon is one of these people. The adrenalin-charged accounting software industry is changing the face of the humble firm. With new technology affecting how accountants run their businesses and interact with their clients, cloud software provides an unprecedented platform of opportunity and innovation. Reading *Remaining Relevant – the future of the Accounting Industry* and implementing new practices will fundamentally change an accounting practice just like the phenomenon of cloud software.
Once you've read Rob's book I'm sure you'll agree, it could have been called 'Remaining Relevant – the Exciting future of the Accounting Industry'."

Julie Benton, General Manager, Wolters Kluwer, CCH New Zealand
New Zealand

"This book is a must read for anyone wanting to take their accountancy business to the next level – it is thought provoking, has a vast number of strategies & ideas and provides an insight into what we should be doing rather than what we are doing.

In reading this book, I suggest you sit down with a highlighter and pen & create an action list of what you need to be doing rather than what you are doing – then go away and create your business by design rather than by default. It will help give you the business and the freedom that you deserve. The accountancy world has changed from the one we all previously knew and will continue to change at a fast pace – make sure you don't get left behind."

Peter Locandro, Partner, ZJL Accounts
Melbourne, Australia

"Rob Nixon has been bringing ideas to the accounting profession for many years. *Remaining Relevant* is one of Rob's biggest contributions to date. If you read it you will take away value added ideas for growing your practice that you won't find so succinctly well packaged anywhere else."

Jay Nisberg, PhD, President, Jay Nisberg & Associates, Inc.
Palm Beach, Florida

"Outsourcing and the 'virtual office' is becoming a way of life for accountants in the know. We have to change what we do and how we think in order to survive. If we want to grow and flourish, we have to get into value added services and break away from time-based billing.

We have to be more selective in which clients we work with, what we do for them and how we bill them. We have to embrace the changes technology offers us as practitioners and fight back! This book offers a roadmap to success for the entrepreneurial accountant, backed up by some pretty thorough and impressive research. If you're running an accounting firm and still want to be in business in five years' time, then you need to read this book."

Steve McIntyre-Smith, Consultant
World's Top Twelve Consultants to the Accounting Profession
(by 'AVN' and 'Build a World-Class Accountancy Practice' in 2013)
Ontario, Canada

Rob Nixon hits it out of the park again with his new book, *Remaining Relevant*. His insights, ideas and information will keep you on the cutting edge of your industry and be way ahead of the pack struggling to be relevant in our fast paced ever changing business world. Rob shares with you easy to implement strategies that will generate a point of difference, that will make all the difference to your bottom line.

Keith Abraham, Author, Passionate Performance
Australia

Rob is a true global thought leader for the accounting profession. Rob understands global trends with local realities. *Remaining Relevant* is a must read for every firm that wants to thrive today and into the future.

Shannon Vincent, Co-Founder ReNew Group
Oakland, California

Rob in his book *Remaining Relevant* has unlocked the vault to understanding how to succeed in an accounting firm and where today's accountant needs to be in the future. This is a must read for any accounting firm.

Mark Holton Director, Smithink 2020
New South Wales, Australia

As an accountant with over 15 years' experience, the groundswell of change that our industry is currently experiencing is unprecedented. The importance of *Remaining Relevant* and being able to move to a true business advisor with our client's is a cornerstone to the future success of our business and the industry. Rob has managed to capture the current threat to our profession and detail what needs to occur now to ensure survival. It is really time to Evolve or Die. *Remaining Relevant* will be a useful guide for us in helping to manage this change now and into the future.

Troy Townley, Co-Founder and Business Advisor - HTA Advisory
Melbourne, Australia

"Rob Nixon has long been at the forefront of predicting the future of the accounting profession and then creating systems, content, hard-hitting advice and more latterly, cloud based technology to help accountants confront the challenges facing them head on, to set themselves up for a bright future in a rapidly changing environment. Rob's new book, *Remaining Relevant*, pulls together thousands of hours of research, study trips, and consultation with hundreds of accounting firms and their clients. He has a unique ability to look in from the outside - the fact that Rob is not an accountant himself enables him to provide his real life expertise as an entrepreneur and successful business owner to help accountants shake off 'the way we have always done things' and create a new approach for the modern world. All accountants in public practice need to immerse themselves in Rob's work. Every chapter of *Remaining Relevant* contains brand new, never seen before content that, when implemented, will place you at the forefront of this great profession of ours."

Colin Dunn ACA (England and Wales), best-selling Author of
'Accountants - the natural trusted advisor' and creator of
TRUST and PANALITIX
Brisbane, Australia

Rob's book *Remaining Relevant* mirrors BGL view on the future of the accounting profession. If Australian accountants are going to remain relevant, in the future they need to review their business models and processes before the world, technology and their clients pass them by. Being an ostrich is no longer an option.

Ron Lesh, Managing Director, BGL Corporate Solutions Pty Ltd.
Victoria, Australia

Rob Nixon has again recorded a timely and astute assessment of the major trends, challenges and opportunities that face the accounting industry today. *Remaining Relevant* is a compelling read and frankly, if you are an accountant, NOT reading

Chapter Three may be harmful to your wealth. Beyond being a succinct industry commentary *Remaining Relevant* should also be used as a practical 'How To' guide for those folks wishing to build profitable and client-centric accounting businesses."

Dave Birch, Founder & Managing Director,
Get Smart Group - feeSmart/feeLink/smartAR
Auckland, New Zealand

"Rob Nixon is visionary about accountancy. The threats of digital disruption for accountants are no longer a theoretical story but are already visible. The tsunami of change can't be ignored and his latest book, *Remaining Relevant*, is literally a survival manual for accountants. For many accountants this book can be their lifeline to success."

Drs. Marcel Spoelstra RA,
Accounting firm Spoelstra & Scherer
The Netherlands

"*Remaining Relevant* will be the most important business book that you read in 2015. We have ordered the first 100 copies for our team. Having practiced as an accountant for 47 years, I believe Rob is 100% on the money with his 12 predictions, ignore them and his action plan at your own peril!"

Anthony S Bongiorno BCom, FCPA, CFP, FIPA, CTA, SSA, Cert IV FMB
Founding Partner, The Bongiorno Group
Melbourne, Australia

"*Remaining Relevant* is a must read for all accounting firms who are serious about being a 'Firm of the Future'. Rob's insights have been changing the lives and success of many accounting firms for years, and this book will assist the next evolution of accounting firms. If you don't take this information on board and implement it using these easy to use strategies, be prepared to die and be left behind by the new modern, mobile, cloud based accountants who can deliver their services in real time. Another brilliant book from Rob Nixon."

Nicholas Sinclair – CEO, The Outsourced Accountant
The Philippines

"In the 8 years I have known Rob he has always been 2 or 3 steps ahead of the Accounting Profession. Identifying the big issues that the Accounting profession face long before most Accountants do. *Remaining Relevant* is no exception. *Remaining Relevant* has summed up the big issues that are either having an impact on the industry and more importantly about to have an impact. Offshoring, Technology, Productizing, Real Time and of course People. It is a thought provoking even confronting but none the less essential read if Accountants are going to thrive in this new era."

Marc Loader, Director, Verve Group
Northern Territory, Australia

"Nobody clarifies the challenges facing the public accounting profession better than Rob Nixon. *Remaining Relevant* offers inspiring insights into the opportunities facing the most trusted advisor, the accountant, to their SMB clients. Being relevant is critical but the real challenge and opportunity is to be empowered to advise and assist in growing successful businesses. *Remaining Relevant* indeed empowers, inspires and motivates. Read and 'just do it'!"

Mike Chisholm, Accountant and Founder
iFirm practice management software

"Rob Nixon is the constant 'breath of fresh air' that the accounting industry needs. Through his years of experience of advising accountants on best practice, he has helped practices achieve goals they never thought possible. His book *Remaining Relevant* is just another example of how in sync Rob is with the industry."

Alan Osrin, Managing Director – Sage Software Australia
Sydney, Australia

"Rob is both confronting and compelling. The writing is on the wall and it appears to be a game changer. Well worth reading."

Ray Taggart, Principal, Taggart Partners
Brisbane, Australia

"This book is incredible. It sums up the current state of the accounting profession and gives a very practical way of rising to the challenges presented by a fast-changing world. My own research in the UK shows that new technology and the rise of the cloud is changing everything. Fast. We need to keep ahead of the curve to ensure we don't go the way of the dinosaur."

Mark Wickersham FCA, #1 bestselling author of
'Effective Pricing for Accountants'
United Kingdom

"Rob Nixon in his new book pushes the accounting profession to reimagine what it means to be a trusted adviser."

Brett Kelly, Founder, Kelly+Partners Chartered Accountants
Australia

"Rob Nixon's new book is a real tour de force – insightful, challenging, helpful – written with his usual brash, no holds barred enthusiasm. He is passionate. He is disruptive. Read this book. It will likely rock your world."

Chris Frederiksen, CPA, CGMA
Chairman and CEO, 2020 Group USA
United States of America

"When Rob Nixon talks about the future of Accounting Profession, I listen and every accountant should too. He doesn't do it to scare you, he does it because he wants you to be still be in business in the future and not a dinosaur".

Phil Richards – Award Winning Entrepreneurial Accountant,
Author and Speaker
Brisbane, Australia

REMAINING RELEVANT

The Future of the Accounting Profession

Rob Nixon

Writing a book of this caliber is a team effort. To the many clients whom I have tormented and cajoled as I tested my ideas and cunning plans, I thank you. To my amazing team who put up with my changing mind and relentless pursuit of better, I thank you. To my business partner, Colin, who is so smart and perfectly aligned to me, I thank you. To my beautiful wife, Nat and 3 awesome kids, you have been so flexible and supportive, I thank you and love you. And a special thank you to my daughter Hattie. The release date of this book is on your 15th birthday. Happy Birthday darling. XOXO.

- Rob

ISBN: 978-1-925209-63-1
Published by VIVID Publishing
P.O. Box 948, Fremantle
Western Australia 6959

Cataloguing-in-Publication data is available from the National Library of Australia

Table of Contents

Chapter 10 – It's all about you

Dear Accountant

Dear Accountant,

I have been privileged to be working with and advising the Accounting profession since May 1994. I was 25 when I started working with you. I am not an Accountant (I left school when I was 16) yet I have gravitated toward your profession. Over the years I have delivered seminars, coaching programs, created DVD training programs, created software, online content, trained thousands and visited hundreds and hundreds of Accountants offices. I have dedicated 20+ years and counting to your profession.

Anyone would think I liked Accountants! I do.

It's a wonderful profession to be working with, yet I see some massive changes happening around the world.

It's all about your industry being 'disrupted.' It's a word (disruption) we hear a lot about these days. We live in a world of disruption. Industries all over the world are being disrupted by technological advancements, social change and innovative thinking.

> Quotable quote:
>
> *"Industries all over the world are being disrupted by technological advancements, social change and innovative thinking."*

Entrepreneurial thinking is being applied to these industries that have been in existence for many decades. A new nimble player will enter the market and challenge the status quo. Typically they will use internet-based technology to 'cut out' parts of the supply chain and give a better experience to the consumer. They will invent better ways of doing something and find cheaper labor to deliver the service or product.

All over the world the industry types that are getting disrupted in a major way are:
1. Intermediaries & supply chain
2. Information providers
3. Processing companies
4. 'Behind a computer' companies

Sound like anyone we know? Hmmm.

Yes – it's you! The Accounting profession globally is being disrupted right now and most Accountants don't even know it is happening.

> Quotable quote:
>
> *"The Accounting profession globally is being disrupted right now and most Accountants don't even know it is happening."*

There are 3 main areas that are being disrupted in the Accounting profession:
1. Compliance is being commoditized by technology
2. Labor is being sourced from less expensive countries
3. Clients are using the internet for your advice

These 3 market forces will only escalate, and if you do nothing about it revenue, profit and business value will erode.

Let's look at each one and work out what you can do to capitalize on each one.

Disruptive area #1 – Compliance is being commoditized by technology

The adoption of Internet (commonly called cloud) based technology is growing at a rapid rate of knots. You can't stop this happening. There is social behavior/change in action (people want to access their information on their handheld device) and there are massive technology companies investing huge sums of money to drive the change – if they don't they won't be in business.

The applications that are used over the Internet are very sophisticated, very accurate and can connect to other Internet systems. For example the Accounting system can connect to the client management system, which can connect to the stock control system and the distribution system. At the client end, inexpensive applications can 'talk to each other' and give real time information to the business leader.

> Quotable quote:
> "The adoption of Internet (commonly called cloud) based technology is growing at a rapid rate of knots."

Here's an example in action:

A customer buys a product / service by whatever means. It is scanned using the bar code and automatically registers the sale into the online accounting system. Bank accounts, income statements and balance sheet data are automatically updated. The action also updates the inventory management system that there is one less product. The client management system (assuming the customer used a login/user name/loyalty card to identify the customer) and the buying habits of that customer are updated and now can be tracked. A real time report / dashboard is automatically updated/sent and the leadership of the business can see the trends or reports immediately on their smartphone or tablet. They might be on a private island at the time sunning themselves and the report comes through or they can check when they choose.

> Quotable quote:
> "No waiting.
> No people.
> All real time.
> All automated."

This level of automation (all driven through the Internet) enables the business leader to make instant management decisions and run a better business. It's happening right now. No spreadsheets manually updated. No paper filing and updating. No need for a meeting to tell me the numbers. No waiting. No people. All real time. All automated.

It's exciting and it is happening right now. In my business I have had this level of automation for 2 years.

Let's look at the accounting process.

Previously it used to be on a spreadsheet, server or hard drive and kept at the client's premises. A bookkeeper (or spouse of the owner) did the data entry using manual key strokes. At the end of the year a file was saved and sent to the Accountant with supporting information. There would be questions and queries back and forth and the Accountant would then prepare a 'set of accounts' and present back to the client some 2-9 months after the initial data was received. The preparation of the historical data was a necessary evil as it had to be done to comply with the government authorities.

However, the data was old data. It was redundant. What help is it when you tell me *'I should have done this and that'* 9 months after the fact? No help whatsoever!

Enter Internet-based accounting systems. The products available offer real time information that do not need people to do the data entry. With these systems the data is more accurate (super computers are doing the processing, not people) and there are less mistakes. As well as that, the accounting systems are offering excellent reporting and data analytics which were only previously offered by Accountants as a management accounting package. The revenue I used to spend with the Accountant, is now delivered by technology.

> Quotable quote:
>
> *"The revenue I used to spend with the Accountant, is now delivered by technology."*

Also because the information is more accurate and the systems only have one version, the time spent at your end to prepare annual accounts is far less. In fact we are seeing anything from 30% to a 60% time reduction at the Accountants' end (in year 2 onwards) for accounts preparation work. What do you do with that time saving? Do you reduce your price? Unfortunately for you, the technology companies are directly promoting that 'You will be more efficient working with your Accountant when you buy our product.' You have been selling 'hours' for all these years and more efficiency means fewer hours and fewer hours should mean a cheaper price. That's what the business community is thinking.

We are seeing more price pressure on compliance than ever before and it will only escalate.

As an example, the New Zealand accounting profession is one of the world leaders in the adoption of cloud accounting technology. They have been active in the space since 2010 and approximately (at the time of writing) 25% of New Zealand small businesses use a cloud accounting product.

As a result of technology and market forces, the New Zealand Accounting profession has been negatively affected. In short, it's going backwards.

All you have to do is take a look at my profit per partner analysis below of the last 11 years. In 2004 the actual median profit per partner was NZ$176,163. In 2014 the actual median profit per partner is NZ$190,409. Not only has the actual profit per partner declined in the past 8 years (from a high of NZ$229,646 in 2007) but when you apply 'CPI plus a bit' of just 5% to each year since 2004 then the 2014 comparison results are staggering.

> Quotable quote:
>
> *"As a result of technology and market forces, the New Zealand profession has been effected. In short, its going backwards."*

The other numbers of Work in Progress, Receivables, Write offs / Realization, Average Hourly Rate and Productivity / Utilization have gone up, down and sideways. At the end of the day it's the profit per partner that matters.

Every expense in a firm is increasing. Salaries and overheads are increasing and you should be running a better firm each year so applying 5% per year profit growth is a very conservative growth target. Based on 5%, the median profit per partner in 2014 should be NZ$286,951.

Alas, this year it's only NZ$190,409. That's almost a NZ$100,000 difference per partner!

How can the average partner in New Zealand afford private school education, decent cars, reasonable holidays and still give back to the community? Most can't.

And to make matters worse, isn't the Accounting profession supposed

> Quotable quote:
>
> *"Most partners are making less than their clients yet they are advising them about business success!"*

to be "The Trusted Advisor" – the "Primary Business Advisor"? Most partners are making less than their clients yet they are advising them about business success! Hmmm.

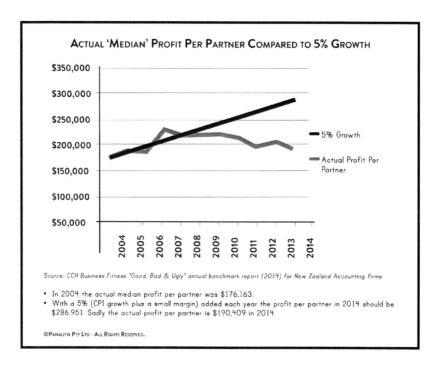

ACTUAL 'MEDIAN' PROFIT PER PARTNER COMPARED TO 5% GROWTH

Source: CCH Business Fitness "Good, Bad & Ugly" annual benchmark report (2014) for New Zealand Accounting firms

- In 2004 the actual median profit per partner was $176,163.
- With a 5% (CPI growth plus a small margin) added each year the profit per partner in 2014 should be $286,951. Sadly the actual profit per partner is $190,409 in 2014.

©Panalitix Pty Ltd - All Rights Reserved.

So why is this happening? I think there are 3 primary reasons:

1. Cloud accounting technology is driving efficiencies in the firm and the profession has been forced to reduce prices.
2. Savvy clients have more information than ever before and they are asking more 'price' and 'value' related questions.
3. Nimble Accounting firms are promoting bundled and cheaper prices than ever before and thus 'commoditizing' compliance.

There is more of this to come. To counteract these market forces the profession has not acted fast enough in marketing, value pricing and delivering business advisory services.

As the old saying goes "if nothing changes, nothing changes." What that means is if you do nothing (strategy, process, tools, etc.)

then nothing changes. In this case doing nothing means everything changes. And a sharp decline in profit should be enough to motivate the industry to change. Let me add one more to the mix before we get onto solutions. **One click lodgment.** With all the Internet data (which is much more accurate) already in the Internet accounting system, how long will it be before the government authorities get their systems ready and allow direct lodgment? The government

> Quotable quote:
>
> *"The reason the majority of the Accounting profession exists is to make sure that the government gets the correct amount of tax money that it is owed."*

authorities do not care about the intermediary called an Accountant. All they want is their tax money! The reason the majority of the Accounting profession exists is to make sure that the government gets the correct amount of tax money that it is owed.

One click lodgment is not far away and it will bypass Accountants and eliminate a big chunk of their revenue.

Technology is disrupting the industry and there is more to come. Is your firm ready?

Disruptive area #2 – Labor is being sourced from less expensive countries

Manufacturing companies have been using low cost labor in developing countries for decades to produce their products. Just look at the clothes on your back. I bet very few of them are made in your current country!

The reality is that (because of escalating labor costs) most western countries have priced themselves out of markets by attempting to produce the product locally.

Up until a few years ago it was primarily 'hardware' based manufacturing companies using this resource. Now we are seeing 'services' companies embrace the outsourcing trend with fully resourced teams.

> Quotable quote:
>
> *"Now we are seeing 'services' companies embrace the outsourcing trend with fully resourced teams."*

Most people think of this as outsourcing where in actual fact the correct term is offshoring.

Outsourcing is where you get someone else to do the task who does not exclusively work for you. Accountants are a classic outsourced service. You work for many clients and they send their work to you because you are better at it than them.

Offshoring is where you set up a team (maybe starting with one person) offshore and they exclusively work for you. The banks and airlines have been doing this for years. They get themselves an office in a developing country, fill it with desks/chairs/computers/phones and hire and train some people, and voila, they have an office that can support their customers.

For one off projects, outsourcing is the way to go, however for larger ongoing tasks offshoring is the way to go.

Accountants have recently embraced the idea very quickly and are hiring people in developing countries with some degree of vigor right now.

I went on an offshoring study tour (in the Philippines) and the opening speaker said 2 things to me that got me excited:

1. *"Any job that can be done over the phone or behind a computer we can do for 50% - 90% cheaper, faster and often better"*
2. *"I have been a virtual assistant for 5 years for a university professor in New York. I have gotten to know her job so well that I now mark her students' papers for her"*

I thought WOW. There are smart, hard workers, there is an abundance of them and they are relatively inexpensive.

> **Quotable quote:**
>
> *"Any job that can be done over phone or behind a computer we can do for 50% - 90% cheaper, faster and often better."*

If you think about an Accountant's day. Most of it is spent on the phone or behind a computer. Most of the day is spent dealing with client queries and processing Accounting work. The technology products will take a lot of the processing work away and the balance can be done by cheaper labor offshore.

What is left are team members who are customer facing and adding value. The Accounting firm of the future has a local team who are customer facing (nurturing, sales and advice) and everything else (back office and processing) is done offshore.

Quotable quote:

"The Accounting firm of the future has a local team who are customer facing (nurturing, sales and advice) and everything else (back office and processing) is done offshore."

There are 3 compelling reasons why this makes sense:

1. An abundance of labor
2. A labor force who are supremely qualified
3. A lower cost structure

Let's take the Philippines as a case in point. It is estimated that circa 1.3M work in this space. It is growing every day. Their English is fantastic, the schooling system is very good, they are very family orientated, the time zones are reasonable and the government is right behind the initiative with infrastructure. They cannot build the office towers fast enough.

The table below highlights the salaries (March 2014) that Accountants in the Philippines are being paid. These are considered 'middle class' salary levels as the cost of living is so inexpensive.

ACCOUNTANTS SALARIES IN THE PHILIPPINES

QUALIFICATIONS / EXPERIENCE	ANNUAL SALARY PH PESO*	ANNUAL SALARY USD$	PER HOUR USD (1800 HRS)
Newly Grad Accounting (non CPA)	P130k – P156k	$2,880 - $3,800	$1.59 - $1.89
Accountant (non CPA) few Years Experience	P182k – P260k	$3,960 - $5,670	$2.19 - $3.15
CPA Accountant (just qualified)	P234k – P286k	$5,130 - $6,210	$2.84 - $3.44
CPA Accountant (5 years experience + can supervise)	P286k – P390k	$6,210 - $8,550	$3.44 - $4.74
CPA Accountant (CFO, Head of Audit level)	P390k – P585k	$8,550 - $12,780	$4.74 - $7.09

* These salaries are what the team member is paid
* Plus BPO (Business Process Outsourcing) "seat fee" costs of approx. USD $500 - $750 per person per month

You can set this model up one of 3 ways:

1. Hire people directly who work from home.
2. Go through a serviced office business (called a BPO) and hire the people through them.
3. Incorporate a company and set up your own office – viable if you need 20+ people.

When hiring someone you do it via video conference (Skype®, Google® hangout, GoToMeeting® etc.) and you do it the same way you already do. Place an ad, go through a recruiter, receive resumes, cull them out and hire the best person for the job.

If you go through option 2 then the Business Process Outsourcing (BPO) will

> Quotable quote:
>
> *"Place an ad, go through a recruiter, receive resumes, cull them out and hire the best person for the job."*

help you hire the people. The training is up to you – again via video conferencing or personally. They are your employees and they need to be trained in your systems and your way of doing things. They become part of your team so they need to be treated as such.

> Quotable quote:
>
> *"They are your employees and they need to be trained in your systems and your way of doing things"*

As an example my Australian team had a cooking class the other night. My team in the office in Manila did one on the same night in their city. My Australian team does daily huddles and they Skype in our team every day in the Manila office. What we do in one office we do in another.

Some people have a problem with this idea. *"We must keep the jobs in our country"* I hear. *"What will our Accountants do if we send the work to a team elsewhere"* is also another one. *"What would my clients think"* is a common one. Well, most Accounting firms will have different nationalities employed already in their local offices. What's the difference? You just have a team working for you in a different country in your 'offshore' office.

If you pare the comments often they are either racist or the person saying them has inadequacies and hang-ups that their job can be done by someone else for a 10th of their salary.

All of this is globalization and a change in social behavior. I think the concept got off to a bad start with telemarketing companies calling you at home and you could not understand what they were saying. It also got off to a bad start because the term 'outsourcing' was created and many Accounting firms sent jobs offshore and because the person worked on the job was not working 100% for that firm there was a lot of re-work needed.

As a disruptive trend we are seeing Accountants use the available resource in the following way:

- Hiring marketing people to do the marketing work for the firm. I know of an Australian $4M firm who has 8 marketing team members offshore.
- Hiring client service coordinators to handle data collection and job set up from clients.
- Hiring bookkeepers to do bookkeeping work for clients – and charging clients @ $20 per hour and making a 5 times margin.
- Hiring data integrity people to sort out client data before it gets to the Accountant.
- Hiring technical people who can do 'cloud conversions' and other software help.

> Quotable quote:
>
> *"Hiring bookkeepers to do bookkeeping work for clients – and charging clients @ $20 per hour and making a 5 times margin."*

- Hiring product development people to create product for the firm.
- Hiring administrators to do document scanning, corporate secretarial, debtor collection, filing, etc.
- Hiring Accountants to do the accounting work that does not involve client facing meetings.

Now here is the BIG one.

Businesses are being directly targeted by Accounting firms (offshore or local ones who have an offshore team) offering accounting work from $8 - $25 per hour. This is escalating at a great rate of knots.

As a consumer of accounting services, why would I pay $200 per hour when I can get it for $20 – or less? There has to be some compelling reasons as to why I would continue paying 10 times as much!

> Quotable quote:
>
> "As a consumer of accounting services, why would I pay $200 per hour when I can get it for $20 – or less?"

The profession has to wake up and realize that you cannot maintain your current prices when technology is commoditizing compliance and global markets are offering lower cost labor direct to your clients.

To hold prices you will have to add value, add value and add more value to remain relevant in the future. Accountants will have to offer valuable commentary to the data in front of them and move much more into business advisory services.

My view is that as an Accountant if you are not <u>adding value to the data that is in front of you</u> then your days are numbered!

This is a big disruption to the labour force of Accountants in Western countries. It is also a great opportunity to capitalize on.

The world is changing fast. Are you ignoring it, embracing it or hoping it will go away?

It won't.

Disruptive area #3 – Clients are using the Internet for your advice

It seems we use the Internet for everything we want/need to know!

Addresses/ companies / people / products/ concerts / store opening times / weather / golf handicap / cycling routes / friends' whereabouts (or what they are eating – yuk) and the BIG one...'**how to do**' every-**thing**. The Internet seems to be our first port of call for anything we want to know or find information on.

Whatever happened to the Yellow Pages, asking people personally, the Encyclopedia Britannica or a Catalogue? All (or nearly) GONE! Social behavior is indicating we need(?) to be connected to our device.

And the device rules supreme. A few weeks back I was at an airport lounge and my traveling companions had a 'device bag' full of connected gadgets.

> Quotable quote:
>
> *"Whatever happened to the Yellow Pages, asking people personally, the Encyclopaedia Britannica or a catalogue? All (or nearly) GONE!"*

The world is connected and it is getting more connected every day. Currently we go to our device (pick up a phone or tablet) and tap in the requested search. We can also talk to our device (the annoying Siri in the iPhone® as a good example) and she/he can help us. Or talk to our car and another annoying voice (but very proper diction) will give us directions to your destination.

Does this give us an enhanced human experience? Probably not. But it sure is efficient.

Mobile technology is booming. It's what consumers want. They want information at their fingertips. Tap tap tap and hey presto – I have the answer and now I am an expert.

And that is an issue for anyone in the advice business (aka Accountants!)

Let's say I wanted to learn about borrowing money through my pension scheme to buy a property. I could 'Google' that and find the answer in a few seconds. What if I wanted to work out how to improve the profit of my winemaking business? I could go to a LinkedIn group and discuss that and get an answer. What if I needed a payroll or tax question answered? I can search it

> Quotable quote:
>
> *"What if I needed a payroll or tax question answered? I can search it and go directly to the government portal and get the answer."*

and go directly to the government portal and get the answer.

Uncle/Aunty Google has all the answers, it seems.

Enter IBM.

The IBM super computer 'Watson' is an extraordinary piece of engineering. It can beat humans (really smart ones) at chess and Jeopardy!

(proven) and 'some say' he/she is so smart he knows what the President of any country will say next! OK…I made the last bit up.

You get the idea. Watson is a super smart supercomputer.

IBM have announced this year (2014) to make a >$2BN investment to develop Watson into a useable resource. There are >2,000 people in the Watson team and their job is to integrate Watson into the world. One of the cool ideas is to create 'Watson for business.' Think of it as 'Siri' (iPhone fame) for business. You have a business question, talk to the device and it gives you the answer. BOOM. Great for the user – not so great for you.

You see, Watson is a sponge like a human. It can absorb / disseminate / translate / organize / conceptualize any information and then send it back in a usable format. Pretty much all of the world's 'texts' (as in manuals, books and all forms of content) are accessible on the Internet. But the Internet is a bit of a mess. There is a lot of content to absorb and disseminate. Watson can sort it out and give it back to you in a useable format.

I got interested in Watson a few months back by the following line in a newsletter I received…

"This is the start of the end of professional services as we currently know it"

WOW. WOW and more WOW!

Does that mean the supercomputer can replace the Adviser? For repetitive and systematic information: absolutely YES. And there will be 'an app for that' very soon.

> Quotable quote:
>
> *"This is the start of the end of professional services as we currently know it."*

I don't mean to scare you but I do. This is real and it is happening right now and the Accounting profession is in the firing line for massive disruption. Without notice and appropriate action these 3 'disrupters' have the capacity to wipe out a (BIG) chunk of revenue / profit / business value in the profession…QUICKLY.

How long before a business owner does not need an Accountant at all? How long before billions of dollars of revenue is wiped out of the current Accounting profession?

It's happening right now and to remain relevant as an industry I think there are only 3 solutions:

1. Add value to what you are doing
2. Be proactive with new services
3. Become the 'Real Time Accountant'

> Quotable quote:
> *"How long before a business owner does not need an Accountant at all?"*

This book is all about you combating the inevitable disruption to your industry. I welcome any debate, comments, observations or even words of praise if you feel so inclined!

Enjoy,

Rob Nixon
January 2015, Brisbane, Australia

Contact details:
rob@robnixon.com | rob.nixon@panalitix.com
www.panalitix.com | www.robnixon.com
Twitter - @therobnixon
LinkedIn – therobnixon
Facebook - rob.nixon.969

Chapter 1
The Way of the Dinosaur

Cloud changes everything

I have a theory as to why most clients of an Accounting firm are within a 'driving radius' of the firm. My theory is that way back when(ever) the clients used to travel to the Accountant's office with their 'stuff' (cashbooks, receipts, livestock headcount, paperwork, etc.), they'd get dressed up in their Sunday best for the occasion, have a pleasant conversation about the year that was and then leave.

The Accountant would then process the 'stuff,' communicate any queries by letter/telex/facsimile/phone or courier pigeon, then present to the client for signing (more pleasant conversation unless an unsightly tax bill awaits) and then finish the annual accounts off. They would then lodge/file the annual return with the various government authorities, the client would pay the tax begrudgingly and next year they'd do it all over again.

The only thing that has changed these days is the format of the 'stuff' that arrives. These days most of the incoming information is either scanned and emailed or provided on a portable disk or stick.

Quotable quote:

"The only thing that has changed these days is the format of the 'stuff' that arrives."

The driving radius of the client to Accountant still exists because the data is still heavy. The challenge with heavy data is the version control of the software, human involvement, inconsistency and data integrity. What happens today is when the information finally arrives, the Accountant processing the work will load the stick or the disk into their computer, check the version (damn it, it's a different version), start moving information around, check the other information provided and then realize that there is a bunch of missing information. At some point of time in the future (sometimes weeks after the client has sent in the information) the Accountant will contact the client with what is missing. The client will ignore the message because it's a pain to deal with. The Accountant will get frustrated and shoot off another email to tell them what to send in. Eventually the client will send in some of the missing information – or the wrong information. Several weeks or months have passed by now. The Accountant now has all of the information. They analyze and manipulate the data, produce a draft set of accounts. They send the draft to the client for signing. The client signs, not knowing if it is right or not. The Accountant then lodges the information with the various government authorities. The client gets a tax bill or a refund – more often than not a bill to pay more. They don't understand why there is a bill and said Accountant is not very good at explaining why. The client pays the bill begrudgingly. And all is done until next year.

I'm exhausted just writing about the process. No wonder Accountants take so long to do things. There are 2 primary reasons why it takes so long to do annual compliance work in an Accounting firm:

> Quotable quote:
> *"I'm exhausted just writing about the process. No wonder Accountants take so long to do things."*

1. Archaic systems – such as hard drive accounting & paper
2. Human involvement – data entry and processing at the client end

The Accounting profession around the world has carved out Billions upon Billions of dollars in annual compliance revenue (which is basically history writing) because of heavy data and human involvement.

Most of an Accountant's revenue is data entry, checking and lodging historical data with the government authorities. We have surveyed firms and they tell us nearly 80% of their compliance revenue (which is typically

> Quotable quote:
>
> *"Most of an Accountant's revenue is data entry, checking & lodging historical data with the government authorities."*

80% of all revenue) is data entry, checking and lodging.

Where's the value in that? Yes, a client can learn from the history lesson but our research shows that the business community does not want an Accountant who deals in redundant (historical) data – they want one who is real time. We asked 428 small business owners if they would prefer a 'redundant data accountant' or a 'real time accountant' and 93% wanted a real time one.

What if the entire process could be simplified? What would happen if the human element was minimized and technology took care of the data integrity?

It can. And it's happening right now. Enter lite data. Lite data in the form of Internet data. Commonly called 'cloud computing.'

Lite data is no data. There are no files to send. No paperwork to email. No version control issues and limited human involvement. Just a login that you and the Accountant, has access to.

Imagine if (at your client site) when our client transacted a purchase with a customer (point of sale) that the bar code triggered the warehouse that there was one less item available and that updated the total inventory. At the same time the transaction updated the customer database (often called a CRM system) that the customer had purchased the item and the accounting system also recognized the sale for the day. The accounting system would show the live inventory levels, the cash balance, the revenue and the profit on a real time basis. All of the systems that used to be disparate 'hard drive' or 'heavy data' systems are now 'talking to each other' via the Internet.

That would be pretty cool as the accounting data would now have much more data integrity. There would be much less 'checking' involved at the Accountant's end as the supercomputers would be doing the checking. There would also be much less data processing at the Accountant's end as the supercomputers would be doing the processing.

There would be much less time involved at the Accountant's end because of version control and supercomputers. Less human intervention and better data.

Sound 'Pollyannaish'? Not really. Short of robots doing all the work in the Accountants' office this is exactly what is happening with Accounting firms and their clients all over the world.

You might say that this is a good thing. I think so as well. You'll definitely be more efficient in your dealing with clients if you promote these sorts of systems.

> Quotable quote:
> "There would be much less time involved at the Accountant's end because of version control and supercomputers."

> Quotable quote:
> "You'll definitely be more efficient in your dealing with clients if you promote these sorts of systems."

You'll have far less time on each and every client who has an Internet-based accounting system. However, there is a dark side to this.

And it has everything to do with the way you have charged your clients in the past.

The diagram below shows the real efficiency savings when you convert your clients across to a cloud accounting system. If you had 10,000 capacity hours to the annual compliance work on the old 'heavy data' system and you changed them over to cloud accounting then for the first year about the same volume of hours is needed to produce the annual work. In year 2, you will have around a 15% saving in time needed, and as the years roll on, up to a 60% saving each year after 5 years of having a cloud-based accounting solution. Sometimes it takes less time than 5 years. Because of the data integrity, you are so much more efficient at the Accountant's end.

THE EFFECT OF CLOUD ON COMPLIANCE

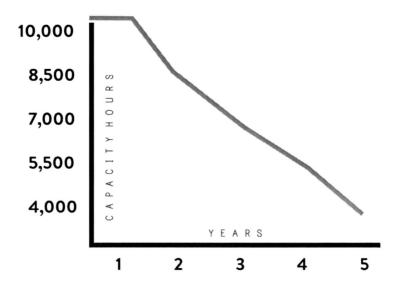

The challenge is what the client expects to pay based on what you deliver. For years the Accounting profession has been promoting 'hourly rates' and 'time'. You have told us, the business community, that you have charge rates, we buy hours and, based on the number of hours and who does the work, the price will be $X.

Because of technology like cloud accounting you have created 'a rod for your own back' when it comes to pricing. Not only can we see that when we use cloud Accounting that it is easier and faster dealing with you but the technology providers are telling us 'when you buy our product you will be more efficient working with your Accountant.' To us, the word 'efficient' means fewer hours needed to do the work. Less hours means less cost.

> Quotable quote:
>
> *"Because of technology like cloud accounting you have created 'a rod for your own back' when it comes to pricing."*

As such, price pressure kicks in about year 2 of using cloud accounting where clients start asking questions about price and value for money. It's an awkward conversation. I know why compliance is so expensive: manual labor, labor costs and archaic systems. It's not like you're making bongo bucks (technical term for a lot) out of compliance. I believe compliance should be value priced accordingly with the value it adds to my financial condition.

The diagram below shows the trend of compliance pricing (pressure and value) based on the time on cloud accounting.

THE EFFECTS OF CLOUD ON COMPLIANCE

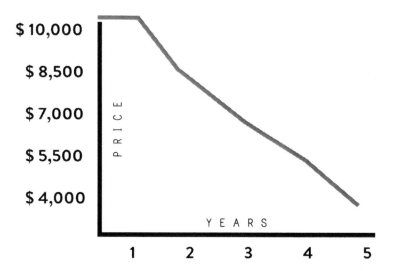

Due to market forces, nimble, marketing-orientated Accounting firms and social behavior compliance will be commoditized and there is nothing you can do about it. We see firms in well developed 'cloud accounting countries' like New Zealand, marketing accounting services for 50% - 80% less than their competitors. They can do this because they have stripped out the cost structure and are using new tools that enable them to be

Quotable quote:

"Due to market forces, nimble, marketing-orientated Accounting firms and social behavior compliance will be commoditized and there is nothing you can do about it."

> Quotable quote:
>
> *"They can do this because they have stripped out the cost structure and are using new tools that enable them to be more efficient in their delivery."*

more efficient in their delivery.

Don't fight it. Instead embrace cloud accounting (promote it hard to all clients) and realize that you now have access to real time data and with the data you can make a real time difference – not a redundant data difference!

Globalization of workforces

The world is flat and getting flatter. No longer do you need to have your team in your office chained to a desk. No longer do you have to hire local labor to get things done.

Take my business as an example. My primary business (www.panalitix.com) is a software company. We provide business advisory software, content and mentoring to Accounting firms around the world. I currently have team members in 4 locations.

To build my software I initially hired 43 programmers in India through 2 BPO's (Business Process Outsourcing) and then when the software was completed (other than enhancements and upgrades) we reduced the team to 6-10 full-time people depending on what we're doing. I have a full-time

> Quotable quote:
>
> *"My team are communicating over Skype™ or Google™ hangouts with each other every day."*

team in the Philippines who do some administration, client service and marketing. My marketing manager lives in Darwin, Australia and I have people in North America as well. My main office is in Brisbane, Australia. All locations are connected via the Internet every day. We run team meetings with web-based video conferencing which costs us nothing. My team are communicating over Skype™ or Google™

hangouts with each other every day. Even our daily 'huddles' (short sharp daily stand up meetings) are run over the Internet. The team work collaboratively using teamwork software. Projects are assigned to a person and that person does what they need to do. If one member of the team has a project that they do not have the expertise on or the current team are busy doing something else they will jump onto Elance.com, oDesk.com or Freelancer.com and find a contractor to get the task done.

Things get done in my business. Fast.

Right now there are millions of contractors around the world who will work for $3, $5, $7 or $10 per hour to do your projects. You can hire a virtual assistant for $3 per hour to do all of your administration work. Anything that can be done behind a computer or over the phone can be done for as little as $3 per hour.

So why don't you use this fabulous resource?

Some Accountants have a moral issue with the world of outsourcing and offshoring. What will my children do? Let's keep the jobs in our country! We hire local! What would our clients think?

Yet what I find interesting about this is pretty much everything you wear is made offshore. Almost everything you buy is made in another country. And to top it all off, the role of an Accountant is to have work outsourced to them!

So you're clients are into it. Why not you!

Here's the dilemma. With the advent of cloud accounting technology, many of the 'low cost labor' countries are getting smart and promoting their services direct to business. They can do the work for a fraction of the cost that you can (in some Asian countries the minimum wage is $1.50 per hour) and often they can do it better and faster.

> Quotable quote:
>
> "With the advent of cloud accounting technology, many of the 'low cost labor' countries are getting smart and promoting their services direct to business"

Almost every firm I meet complains about their people. We can't get enough good quality people. The crew we have aren't very good. They're inefficient and lazy.

So get some new ones and stop whining about it. There is an abundance of good quality Accountants and administration team members in the world – they currently just don't work for you. So go find them and hire them.

Here's another dilemma (wake-up call time) for those Accountants who are currently employed in a firm. I'm talking to the ones who spend a lot of their time doing data entry and processing work. Technology is making the processing work easier and faster. The supercomputers are processing the data via massive 'server farms.' Low cost labor is infiltrating the marketplace. Let me make it really clear…

If you are not going to add value to the client work you are doing, then your $70k, $90k, $120k salary is at risk. Why does a partner need to pay you large sums of money when they can get the same job done for a 1/5th of the price elsewhere?

Employed Accountants who spend their time behind a computer and not communicating with clients will go the way of the dinosaur. The firm of the future has a local team who are client facing and adding value. Everything else is handled by someone else in another location/country. Technology enables globalization of workforces. The world is flat. Get used to it and use it.

> Quotable quote:
>
> *"The firm of the future has a local team who are client facing and adding value. Everything else is handled by someone else in another location/country."*

Compliance as a commodity

> Quotable quote:
>
> *"The Government is using you as an intermediary. They are outsourcing their job to you."*

Statutory compliance or 'have to' annual accounting is mandated by the Government as a task you need to do with your clients. The main reason the Government agencies want you to do this task is so you can accurately (or thereabouts) collect the right amount of money for them. The Government agencies are not that interested in the

Accounting profession. The secondary reason they want you is to check that your clients are complying with their rules.

The Government is using you as an intermediary. They are out-sourcing their job to you.

As a business owner the annual compliance is a necessary evil that we don't really want to buy or really value. It's a grudge purchase. We (the business community) don't like paying for it, we know we have to have it but we just don't like it. It's like filling the car up with petrol. If we could avoid it we would. We can't.

The old model of compliance work is to send a questionnaire to the clients at year end and then wait. Eventually your client sends in their 'stuff' in a variety of formats (paper, scan, email, disk, stick or verbal) and then you make sense of it.

If the information arrived via a file of some sort, the first thing you do is load the USB stick and check the version of their software. You then check the information received versus the information requested. Never the twain shall meet on that one!

Once you realize you do not have the information you requested you go back to the client with an information request (typically by email) and your Accountants then wait. And wait and wait and W... A... I... T

There is no priority to send back the missing information. We sort of know the answer to our finances anyway. It's a grudge purchase so why send it back to you when you want.

> Quotable quote:
>
> *"It's a grudge purchase so why send it back to you when you want.*

Often the communication we get is not very clear when we are requested to send in whatever. We procrastinate sending back the infor-mation because it has little value. And often when we do send it back, you then ask for something else. Why couldn't you have just asked for the complete list in the first place? To make it super easy, why don't you send your administration person around to collect everything?

So we eventually get everything to you. We sign it off, you lodge/file it and the year is done. Next year we do it all over again. Rinse and Repeat. Most of an Accounting firm's revenue is in compliance and it's all about to change.

So what does the future of compliance look like?

There is one word to describe the future of compliance…commoditized. With a repetitive task, eventually systemization kicks in and after that commoditization happens. Once a product is commoditized then price pressure and new competition takes over. This is what is happening with statutory compliance for individuals and companies.

The reason is simple. Cloud accounting software. New technologies at the client's end makes it far more streamlined, accurate and thus efficient. The data received by the Accountant is more accurate and better quality. There are fewer errors to make at the client's end due to the way cloud solutions work. With the data in better shape, that means there is less time needed at the Accountant's end to finalize the work. The software applications also offer reporting that previously only the external Accountants would provide – such as consolidated executive summaries with key performance indicator variances, budgeting and cash flow analysis.

I have recently seen new entrants (Accountants) to the marketplace who have a very low cost base and are offering 50% - 80% reduction on standard compliance work. I am also seeing a growing trend of Accountants setting up teams of people in other countries and offering bookkeeping and other accounting services for $10-$20 per hour.

The next phase will be when the cloud based Accounting systems will offer 'one click lodgment' to the government agencies. This type of technology will bypass the Accountant all-together for these functions. The Australian Government has created 'standard business reporting' linked into the cloud accounting software. They estimate that 12.5% of compliance revenue will be wiped out of the Australian marketplace in the next few years.

> Quotable quote:
>
> *"The next phase will be when the cloud based Accounting systems will offer 'one click lodgment' to the government agencies."*

The reason all of this is happening is due to social change and technology companies who are fighting to remain relevant. Social change says that people want to access information on their mobile device whenever or wherever they want – including accounting and other key business data.

It is hard to do that if all the information is on a hard drive at the office!

Technology companies know this and they are either creating new applications that are Internet based or they are migrating their current 'hard drive' products to be Internet based. If they do not then they will go the way of the dinosaur as well.

Because the cloud data is more accurate and up to date, the version of the software is always up to date and the reporting functions are more powerful, the 'numbers power' is now with your clients in real time. Previously the external Accountant had the numbers power. Previously your voodoo magic, hoketry poketry (hands currently waving in mysterious mystic ways) that you did on a set of accountants was the powerful secret sauce.

Now the technology at your client site is the secret sauce!

If you want to remain relevant you need to regain the numbers power. You need to know what is happening in your client site every day and you need to predict issues and opportunities in advance. You need to be alerted to what is happening so you can react in real time. You can make a massive difference if you have the real time data pushed to your desktop in a consolidated and simple way.

> Quotable quote:
>
> *"Now the technology at your client site is the secret sauce!"*

The Accounting robots will come. The apps with answers will come. But they are a few years off yet. Not as far as you think however.

As an accountant you cannot stop all of this change. Social change, technology companies and the government are creating this change. You can choose to ignore it or embrace it. Ignore at your peril, I say.

12 predictions of the profession

The last time I made 12 predictions on the future of the Accounting profession was in 2010. They were bold predictions and I am happy to report that 66% (8) are done and the other 4 are a work in progress, but happening. The profession has changed a lot mainly due to the new threat and opportunity with cloud computing. So it's time to make another 12 predictions…

1. Compliance will be completely commoditized. Statutory compliance is a repetitive task where 'supercomputers' are taking over the processing and checking of data. Soon enough the tax departments will install standard business reporting and 'one-click' tax lodgment into Internet accounting systems. The Accountant will be bypassed for standard annual reporting in the future.

2. Cloud accounting will be installed in >90% of small to medium size businesses. No one can stop social change. People want their data and information on their mobile devices. No one can stop huge technology companies from heavily promoting their solutions to businesses. It's time to embrace the change.

> Quotable quote:
> *"No one can stop huge technology companies from heavily promoting their solutions to businesses. It's time to embrace the change."*

3. Cloud practice management will be in >90% of Accounting firms. The benefits are clear with improved efficiency, cheaper operating costs and mobility. At some point in time the 'hard drive' providers who also provide cloud solutions will turn off the hard drive updates. It's time to embrace the benefits of change.

4. Coaches and consultants will take more clients. The one who has access to the financial data owns the long term relationship. It is easy for a 'non-Accountant' to help a client get onto cloud accounting and other add-on products. Don't let someone else get more financially intimate with your client than you.

5. Clients will be more transient. One thing that hard drive systems did was make it harder for the client to change Accountants. They had to physically deliver or courier the data to you and thus felt compelled to stay with you. With cloud accounting the data is 'lite' data. There is no data to deliver – just a login. The data can be manipulated anywhere. Tighter and more enduring relationships will be needed.

6. Offshore teams will be more prevalent. With cloud computing why do you need a team of people in your office? Why not look for labor in other countries? Often the labor is cheaper, more accessible and more willing to work. We already have Accounting firms with full-time teams in other countries serving clients around the world.

7. Compliance prices will plummet by 50% or more. Let's face it. Where is the value in a financial report that is 6, 12 or 18 months old? I understand that the labor costs and archaic systems cause the cost of annual compliance to escalate. With new systems I think the costs will come down to where they should be. Compliance should be value priced...down.

> Quotable quote:
>
> *"Let's face it. Where is the value in a financial report that is 6, 12 or 18 months old?"*

8. Marketing and sales skills will be needed. With commoditized services comes price pressure and new low cost entrants into your market. You need to differentiate and make compelling reasons as to why clients should stay with you or move to you. New marketing and sales skills will be needed.

9. Young people will not buy into staid and boring. The old models of 'commander control' management and hierarchical office bound seniors are not what the 20 something's want to sign up for. They are not interested in old-fashioned systems/equipment/furniture/offices and boring restrictions. Loosen up Partners – the next Partners are tech savvy and want to progress faster than ever before. Your firm needs to accommodate this. Maybe we need a reality TV show about Accountants. Maybe we need to 'sex' the industry up a bit. I think so.

10. No more time-based billing. If there was ever a system that denigrated self-esteem and the value of one's knowledge it is time-based billing. It suggests that the time taken was correct and the rate per hour was correct (based on a silly salary multiple formula) to determine the value of the intellectual property. The industry needs to stop this archaic behavior and value the intellect that has taken many years to develop and hone. Price upfront based on value created not time taken in arrears.

> Quotable quote:
>
> *"If there was ever a system that denigrated self-esteem and the value of one's knowledge it is time-based billing.*

11. Business advisory services to be more than 80% of revenue. Accountants can add a huge amount of value when they know the facts. If a client is in trouble they can 'swing into gear' and sort out the situation with the bank or tax department. The problem is that most Accountants are swamped by compliance services and don't have time to add value. That's all changing and with new technologies that alert the Accountant as to what is going on with the client the Accountant can truly live up to the trusted adviser status that they so richly deserve.

12. Clients are finally served properly. It always amazes me that when we give an income statement and balance sheet (of a client) to an Accountant and get them to brainstorm (in small groups) they come up with loads of ideas on what the client can do to improve. Isn't that what it is all about? Helping the clients. With accurate real time data, Accountants can add value like never before. At the end of the day the client is why most Accountants got into this profession in the first place. I think it's a duty of care to serve them well.

> Quotable quote:
>
> *"With accurate real time data, Accountants can add value like never before."*

These predictions are my predictions. They are based on 20+ years of advising just one industry in many countries around the world. I am privileged to be independent from all vendors and associations and my views are based on observation, fact and what works.

My belief is that if you do not step up, be proactive and add value, then many in the Accounting profession will go the way of the dinosaur.

That's it for the doom and gloom. The rest of the book is all about solutions. The Accounting Profession doesn't have to be an industry that is marginalized or made extinct.

Chapter 2
A new plan is needed

Business by Design

Most Accounting firms are operating their **business by default** – not operating their **business by design**.

Most Accounting firms just seem to exist. They get through the years with a limited plan, they seem to 'acquire' a bunch of clients who are 'hotch potch' of make, model and size. They do not typically run the firm like a business, and worst of all the Partners typically operate the firm based on what they learned from the Partners of the firms where they used to be employees.

> Quotable quote:
>
> *"Most Accounting firms are operating their* **business by default** *– not operating their* **business by design.***"*

This beast that you own is a business – not a practice. You own it. You take all the risk. Your name is on legal documents. Your name is on the insurance policies, the credit cards, the loans, the leases. Your entire team will all leave one day (they eventually always do) and you'll still be there. Your clients are in the deal for their annual fee and their work done. Your team members are in it for their salary and career progression. You are in this thing for millions!

This thing that you own is not a community service or a charity. However, many firms like a not-for profit, community-serving establishment taking on clients they don't like, doing work they don't like and dealing with people they don't particularly like either.

Remember, it's your business and no one else's. You should be the benefactor of the spoils and the one enjoying it the most. One of the key purposes of a business is to create wealth for the owners. How's that going for you?

My definition of success is *"doing what you want, when you want, with whom you want in a manner you want."* That's my life success formula. In a business sense...

> **Quotable quote:**
>
> *My definition of success is* **"doing what you want, when you want, with whom you want in a manner you want."**

1. Are you doing the sort of work (100%) you want to do?
2. Are you doing the work when you want to do it? Your terms.
3. Are you working with people (team and clients) who are inspiring, challenging and fun?
4. Are you operating the business in a manner (style) that you want?

My business structure allows me to do all of the above all of the time. It's my business; I designed it my way with what I want to do. You shouldn't be a slave to your business – it should be a slave to you.

It's not too late to take charge and re-model it. The clock of business existence is ticking. If you have 10 years left in your business, that's only 2,000 days. If you've got 20 years left, that's only 4,000 days. It's not much time.

To run a business by design new rules need to be made. Sometimes tough decisions need to be made. New strategies need to be implemented and often new people need to be involved.

As you are re-modeling, there are 5 key areas (in order of priority) that need to be focused on.

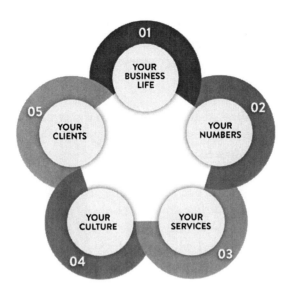

It starts with you designing (or re-designing) your business life. If you had a clean sheet of paper how would you operate on a day-to-day basis? Would you do so many personal chargeable hours? Would you work such long hours? Would you schedule more holidays? Would you be more selective with the

Quotable quote:

"If you had a clean sheet of paper how would you operate on a day-to-day basis?"

clients you are serving? Would you have the operational responsibility that you currently have?

It's your business and it starts with you. Towards the end of every year I schedule the year ahead. I block out all known activities such as…

- ✓ Gym sessions
- ✓ Date nights
- ✓ Bike riding
- ✓ Blog writing
- ✓ Kids drop off
- ✓ School holidays
- ✓ Man-cations
- ✓ Rob & Nat holidays

✓ Unavailable time
✓ Golf – practice & play
✓ Meetings – team, board, forum
✓ Conferences to attend

I then work around what is left. If a client wants me to do something on a Wednesday then I politely decline because that's golf day. How can I do proper work when I am playing golf?

I hired a General Manager to run the day-to-day operations of my software company. I am not that good at day-to-day operations and more importantly I don't like doing it. I only do client work that I want to do for a fee that I think is acceptable. I only speak at events I want to speak at. I work when I want to work. And I work where I want to work. As an aside I am writing this on a Saturday afternoon at Santa Monica Pier in California while having a glass of wine. It's my business.

I think Partners of Accounting businesses should be doing 3 things and 3 things only in their business life:

> Quotable quote:
>
> *"I think Partners of Accounting businesses should be doing 3 things and 3 things only in their business life."*

1. High end chargeable work for the percentage (hopefully low) that lights your fire
2. Sales & nurturing meetings with existing or prospective clients
3. Leadership – driving the performance of the firm, developing new ideas and keeping people accountable

What do you need to change in your business life?

Next come **your numbers**. What do you want them to look like? If you are totally happy with the financial performance of your business then skip this part. Most are not happy with the numbers.

The cool thing about the Accounting profession is that you can create wealth from it. I know of many Partners who make >$2M per year. Not that profit is the most important thing – but hey, it's right up there with breathing!

If you want 1 location or 5 locations, make it happen. If you want your profit before partners salaries to be >60% then make it happen. If you want a $5M, $10M, $100M firm then build it. If you want negative work in progress or receivables then do it. If you want high or low productivity/utilization then make it happen. If you want fewer clients but more revenue per client then

> Quotable quote:
> "The cool thing about the Accounting profession is that you can create wealth from it."

do it. If you want revenue per full time person (including Administration) to be $200K, $300K or $500K then do it.

The neat thing is that all of the strategies already exist on how to improve any number in any Accounting business. Send me an email and I'll email you a free strategy map with 484 projects on exactly how to improve revenue, profit, cashflow and capacity. We've improved the numbers of thousands of Accounting firms over the years.

The numbers can be whatever you want them to be. It starts with a decision.

So you've worked out what your business life and your numbers need to look like. Now you need to focus on **your services** that you want to deliver.

Your government tells you what you have to deliver but is that what you want to deliver? I sell the same thing you do which is intellectual property. We both sell what we know. What do you know and what do you want to sell? How do you want to package that? How do you want to price it?

> Quotable quote:
> "If you don't like doing compliance work but feel you have to deliver it then systemize it, delegate it or send it 'offshore' for someone else to do it."

Studies consistently show that your clients need (and are prepared to pay accordingly if the value is articulated correctly) additional services from you. Your clients do not need more compliance work. They need help with revenue, profit, cashflow, asset protection, succession planning, financial retirement and tax minimization. The compliance work is a necessary evil and a grudge purchase. The business advisory work really helps improve the financial condition of your clients. It's more fulfilling for you and more lucrative as well.

If you don't like doing compliance work but feel you have to deliver it then systemize it, delegate it or send it 'offshore' for someone else to do it. If you want to have more business advisory work in your revenue mix then make that decision and then implement what you need to implement it.

> Quotable quote:
>
> *"You need to develop your operating culture that suits your style, and then find team members who want to operate within that culture."*

Selfishly, the first 3 are about you. Your life, your numbers and your services. Now you need to develop your **operating culture** that suits your style, and then find team members who want to operate within that culture.

In 2010 I had my 'annus horribilis' of a year when it came to team members. I had 27 people movements in a team of 16! Some of the roles were like a revolving door. The culture was bad and I was at fault. As you can imagine it wasn't a great year for team performance. So I decided to do something about it. What I did was write 15 culture standards and 15 service standards. They were standards of behavior. I had documented the behavior I wanted. I documented my culture

I wrote them all first and then I rolled them out via email every 3 days and at the weekly team meeting. I included a description of what each one meant. At the team meeting we did a small workshop on each one. I included them in employment agreements. I got giant banners made, we emphasized them every week, we made them crucial to new team member induction process and slowly the culture started to change.

And we called people on them. Over the years I have had to fire people because they did not live up to the culture standards. We make decisions based on the standards and we live by them every day.

If you would like a copy of my 15 service and 15 culture standards email me and I'll send them to you. What do you need to do to design your culture?

Your business life, your numbers, your services, your culture, and last comes **your clients**. They don't come first. You come first. Your team second and your clients last. I think it is wrong to put the clients first. You're the one taking all the risk – you come first.

I am not saying that you should be arrogant towards your clients or treat them poorly. What I am saying is that you design the business the way you want it to be designed and then find clients to fit that design. Not the other way around!

Most Accounting firms start getting clients by default and more clients and more clients and more clients. Then one day it's like "where did they all come from?".

If you're going to build a business by design then you need to understand who your ideal client is. What do they look like? Where do they hang out? What is their profile? What fees are they paying? What services are they buying? Are they on cloud accounting or can they be moved to cloud accounting? Are they part of your niche focus? Who is your best buyer?

> Quotable quote:
>
> *"If you're going to build a business by design then you need to understand who your ideal client is."*

Now the challenge is that many of your current clients are not your best buyer. Many may have been suitable when you started the firm. Are they suitable now? It is certainly difficult to 'right' your client base in a short space of time. It can be done however. If you make the decision to sell off some of your less than desirable clients then do it. If you make the decision to fire (compassionately) some of your less than desirable clients then do it.

Whatever you do, make sure the next client you accept into your firm is the right client for what you want in the future. If you have an abundance mentality rather than a scarcity mentality then you'll make the tough calls. If you believe that you have the capabilities to gain more clients then why not let a few go?

Business by design is all about designing (or re-designing) the business the way you want it done. If you need to re-design the business then it will take time however it is worth it in the end.

Your clients will be happier, your team will be happier, your family will be happier and most importantly you will be happier.

BHAG's and SMAG's

Most accounting firms set no goals or at best they set small goals. If they do set any goals they set SMAG's – **Small Minded Adequate Goals.**

If you go back to my success formula (doing what you want, when you want, with whom you want, in a manner you want) then a SMAG may be appropriate for your style. At least it's a goal – albeit a goal that doesn't fill your potential.

In my opinion (and this entire book is based on my opinion – plus a lot of research) we're only here once so let's do something purposeful. Let's do something grand. Let's do something that lives beyond us.

Let's set some BHAG's – **Big Hairy Audacious Goals.**

> Quotable quote:
>
> *"A BHAG can inspire you, your team and your clients."*

The term BHAG was first used by Jim Collins in his landmark book 'Good to Great'. A BHAG can inspire you, your team and your clients. The great American President, John F Kennedy, had an awesome BHAG that inspired a nation and many people around the world:

"By the end of this decade we will put a man on the moon and bring him back safely."

Now that's a BHAG. Now apparently it did happen. Either way it got people excited and hundreds of millions of people watched in excitement in July 1969 as Neil Armstrong and Buzz Aldrin walked on the moon and then returned safely to this planet.

What then followed was space exploration, new research, new industries and now (at the time of writing) there are at least 3 wealthy Entrepreneurs building and testing spacecraft to take the regular public to suborbital space. I am one of those 'Future Astronauts' where at some time in the future I will be flying on Virgin Galactic into space. My wife bought me my ticket in 2009 for my 40th birthday. Pretty cool gift and pretty cool wife!

BHAGs for an Accounting firm come in many shapes and sizes.

The BHAG could be revenue related "*$10M in Revenue in 10 years.*" It could be team member related "*100 of the best, brightest and most creative Accountants on the planet.*" Or it could be client related "*All of our 500 clients are financially retired.*"

Whatever the BHAG is, it needs to be bold, it needs to inspiring and it needs be easily communicated. It needs to get you excited and it needs to get the team excited.

Before the BHAG is your purpose and your mission. Why is it you do what you do? What's your purpose for being? Why do you go to work every day? Why do you care so much about your clients? As bestselling author and TED star, Simon Sinek, would say "*people don't buy what you do, they buy why you do it.*"

> Quotable quote:
>
> *"Whatever the BHAG is, it needs to be bold, it needs to inspiring and it needs be easily communicated."*

Some examples you may want to R&D...rip off and duplicate.

Purpose: Making a massive difference to clients' financial performance
Mission: Help all of our clients to financially retire
BHAG: By 2020, 100% of our current clients are financially retired

Or...

Purpose: Helping all clients achieve all of their goals
Mission: Provide every service to every client that helps them achieve their goals
BHAG: $10M in revenue from 400 Awesome clients

> Quotable quote:
>
> *"I particularly like a client-focused purpose, mission and BHAGs."*

I particularly like a client-focused purpose, mission and BHAGs. And the reason for that is you can promote it to the clients. You can use it in your marketing. Let's say you're talking to a new prospective client. The conversation might go something like this:

"At our firm we help our clients achieve all of their goals. We make sure that every single client is only buying what they need from us to help them achieve their goals. We're only looking for 400 awesome clients who want our help to achieve their goals. Tell me, Bob, what are you looking for in an Accounting firm?"

Unless Bob is a complete 'nuff nuff' (technical term for not a very good client) then he's probably going to answer with *"An Accounting firm that helps me achieve my goals."* Sale made. Rinse and repeat.

Get creative with this. Start with what you (the owner) wants then involve your team. Some of your team members have some super ideas. Ask them individually why they became Accountants. Ask them what 'juices' them up. Ask them what they want from their careers. Ask them what they would do if they were running the firm. Get to a consensus. Then do a reality check and see where you are today with your Purpose, Mission and BHAG.

> Quotable quote:
> *"Ask them what 'juices' them up. Ask them what they want from their careers. Ask them what they would do if they were running the firm."*

After that it's action time. If you want a different result (BHAG) then you have to make some different decisions and then Action those decisions. Decision + Action = Result.

For my business advisory software company (**www.panalitix.com**) we are very clear what our purpose, mission and BHAG are. They help us make decisions and help us keep on track.

Purpose: Positively influencing lives through Accountants
Mission: Make Accountants real time
BHAG: 10,000 'Real Time' Accounting firms using PANALITIX every day

What's your purpose, mission and BHAG? When you're done, send it to me. I'd love to see what you come up with.

Breaking with in order to breakthrough

My good buddy, Michael Sheargold, has a fabulous saying: *"Often a breakthrough happens after a break with."*

I love it. If you look at making progress often there is something in the way of achieving that progress. So if you want the result bad enough 'break with' whatever is in the path.

Over the years I have seen many firms break with many things. I have seen firms break with people who are unwilling to change. I have seen firms break with clients who are just downright rude, obtuse and hard work. I have seen firms break with systems, processes, technology, methods, furniture, workflow procedures and pricing models. And I have seen firms break with business partners!

I once did a TEDx talk about success and one of the points was on toxic relationships. Why put up with toxic, energy sucking, demoralizing, uninspiring people was the essence of it. Get rid of them I said. Life is too short. I was hosting my annual conference and a partner of a firm who I hadn't seen for a while approached me the minute he got there and said:

"I listened to your TED talk 3 weeks ago and what you were saying about toxic relationships really hit home. So I left my wife the next day!"

Whatever it is that is holding you back. Break it. You'll be happier when you do. When you do break with it, consider having some fun with it and having a *'breaking with ceremony'*.

Recently I was operating 2 brands in the Accounting profession. There was confusion in the office and confusion in the marketplace. I was confused sometimes. We decided to do something about it. On October 17 2014 we got rid of one brand. But we didn't do it quietly. We burned the brand we didn't want to keep. When I say burned I mean burned. We had a burning ceremony with a fire drum and burned the

> Quotable quote:
> *"If you look at making progress often there is something in the way of achieving that progress."*

> Quotable quote:
> *"But we didn't do it quietly. We burned the brand we didn't want to keep."*

old brand…literally. We had the entire team + 35 clients watching on. I gave a short speech, everyone had champagne in hand and then I set fire to anything that had the old brand on it. There was black billowing smoke coming out of the fire drum and it lasted for close to 2 hours in our office parking lot. It's a wonder the fire department wasn't called.

To make some more noise we sent out media releases. We sent out emails and letters to announce the burning. We had the national press pick up on the story and it featured the following Wednesday covering 1/3 of the page in the most prestigious financial newspaper in Australia. Let's face it, it was a brand makeover. Brand makeovers are not very exciting reading and don't make the press very often. We were picked up online and even a number of interviews were had.

If you're going to go to the trouble of breaking with something. Make some noise about it.

The issue with all of this is you and your motivation. Do you want the result bad enough? If you have business partners, do they want the result bad enough? People are generally motivated by fixing pain or achieving pleasure. What pain do you want to fix and what pleasure do you want to achieve?

I heard a saying at some seminar once *'if the dream is big enough the facts don't count.'* I don't entirely agree with everything regarding the facts – we need facts. However, the context of the saying is if your reasons are big enough then you'll do whatever it takes to make it happen.

> Quotable quote:
>
> *"If the dream is big enough the facts don't count."*

When it comes to 'breaking with,' are your reasons strong enough? Do they motivate you? Are you prepared to do what it takes? Hopefully everything you read in my Dear Accountant letter and everything in chapter one is enough to motivate you to action.

Chapter 3
The Real Time Accountant

Redundant or Real Time

The vast majority of Accountants I meet are offering 'Redundant Data' advice. They are offering up information based on old data. Clients don't want services that are late. They want 'Real Time' services that are on time, relevant and pre-emptive.

Where is the value offering advice that is late? Picture the scene. You are doing your client's annual Accounting and you spot some anomalies or issues from the previous year. You finish off the work and then write a letter to the client explaining what they should do to fix it!

What they should do! Seriously, it's typically too late.

I know you have a duty of care to tell the client the issue – and you did that. Well done you. But it's still late.

With today's accounting technology (on the Internet) you can know what is going on all the time. You don't need to know all the detail - just enough to spot issues and opportunities. Your clients are not Accountants and you have an uncanny knack of seeing financial data and making it make sense to them.

You can even have the data consolidated into single 'dashboards' so you can get a summary of all your clients affairs on one page. Then the technology can alert you to the good and the bad issues

> Quotable quote:
>
> *"You can even have the data consolidated into single 'dashboards' so you can get a summary of all your clients affairs on one page."*

only. With this sort of technology you can pre-empt issues and advise the clients accordingly. Now that's adding value.

It's all about becoming a Real Time Accountant not a Redundant Data Accountant. It's all about being Proactive and not reactive. Real Time Accountants' behave differently and they are much more client focused. The table below highlights some of the behavior.

REDUNDANT OR REAL TIME	
Redundant Data Accountants	**Real Time Accountants**
Offers advice late or not at all	Offers advice before it happens
Processes work and administration	Value added services that help
Waits for things to happen	On front foot making it happen
Majority of revenue in compliance	Majority of revenue in advisory
Prices in arrears	Prices every project upfront
Doesn't visit / call me	Visits and calls on systematic basis
Doesn't follow up	Follows up on every opportunity
Doesn't promote the latest thing	Always promoting
Most clients on 'hard drive' accounting	Most clients on 'cloud' accounting
Numbers power with the client	Numbers power with the Accountant

Let's break each one down and see what they mean:

Offers Advice late or not at all vs. Offering advice before it happens.

Offering advice after the fact and late really does not help anyone. Conversations that start with 'what you should have done is' or 'next time do this' or 'can you tell me what this means' are conversations that are about to offer little or no value. Instead why not preempt what is going on with the client. Be on the front foot spotting trends and anomalies before they happen. Let your client know that you have noticed (for example) that receivables are up, payables are up and inventory is too high. Let them know that they are probably in for a cashflow

> Quotable quote:
>
> *"Real Time Accountants are analyzing data as it happens and offering real time advice."*

grind. Let them know that you can help fix it. Now that's being proactive. With cloud accounting and predictive analytical software you can do this. Real Time Accountants are analyzing data as it happens and offering real time advice.

Processes work and administration vs. Value added services that help.

There is a lot of administration work in compliance. A lot of data entry, checking data and ultimately filing. I know that the filing of tax returns and annual financial statements is mandated by Governments around the world. It's a necessary evil that we have to buy. We don't want to buy it yet we have to buy it. A bit like fuel for your car. It's a grudge purchase. There is a lot of processing work to be done yet there is little value in it for your client. It is all based on historical data that I, the client, cannot change. As a business owner I want the 'good stuff'. I want the help that actually helps me improve my financial condition. I want services that create a tangible return for me. Real time Accountants are always finding new services that offer more value to the client.

Waits for things to happen vs. On the front foot making it happen.

Accountants are world leaders in waiting. If there was an Olympic gold medal for the industry that waited for things to happen then most Accountants would probably win every year with no competitors! Redundant Data Accountants wait for the Government to change the rules and then they offer more services. They wait for the phone to ring, the email to ping. They wait for the bank to tell them that their client is in trouble. They wait for team members to complain. They wait and wait and wait for missing information to be sent back from their clients. They spend most of their professional waking hours....WAITING. Real Time Accountants are on the front foot making it happen. They are creating their own story, their own future. They are not waiting for the Government to marginalize their services by developing 'Standard Business Reporting' (this is

> Quotable quote:
>
> *"Real Time Accountants are very proactive, making things happen and not waiting for things to happen."*

happening in Australia right now where it is estimated that $500M of annual compliance will be eliminated because of SBR) nor are they waiting for clients to send back missing information when they are ready. No. Real Time Accountants are very proactive, making things happen and not waiting for things to happen.

The majority of revenue in compliance vs. Majority of revenue in business advisory.

Having 60%, 70% or 80% plus of your revenue tied up in compliance is your choice. No one's decisions or actions except your own has given you the burden of a great amount of your revenue tied up in Redundant Data Accounting services. If you truly believe that your clients want to buy business advisory services then do something about it. Many firms have systemized the function of compliance so that they can be more efficient and create capacity. Many firms have automated the compliance process so that they have capacity to deliver business advisory. Many firms are actively promoting business advisory services to their clients. Many firms are 'offshoring' compliance work so they have the capacity with the current team to deliver business advisory. It starts with the will to change then the decisions to be made and then actions to be taken. The true Real Time Accountants are making business model decisions and turning the percentage around (of compliance to business advisory) so they have much more revenue in business advisory versus compliance.

Prices in arrears vs. Prices every project upfront.

The old way of pricing was to work out how much time was spent on the client job and apply an hourly rate to the time and then multiply hours X rate. And hey presto a price is derived. Imagine if a client came to you and said, *"Oh, wise Accountant, I have a new product idea and I would like some advice on how much I should charge for it."* And you respond with: *"Here at the Accounting firm this is how we would price it. We would take the total salary of the person creating the product and divide that number by 1,700 working hours. That would give us salary price per hour. We would take that number and multiply it by 4 times and that would give us a charge rate for the person doing the work. Then we would divide that number by 10 so we had a 'unit price' for every 6 minutes of work. Then as the person is creating the product we would have them record how many units of time it took them to create the product. At the end we would multiply the units (time taken) by the unit price and voila we would have the price."* At this point in time your client is logically

> Quotable quote:
>
> "The ONLY legitimate way to price a product or service is to see what the market is prepared to pay for it."

wondering if the marketplace would pay that price, if the person doing the work is efficient or not or if the salary level is correct in the first place. The ONLY legitimate way to price a product or service is to see what the market is prepared to pay for it. You do that by putting your offering to the market (with a fixed price upfront) and see how readily they buy it at your offered price. If they say 'yes' without hesitation then your price is too low. Real Time Accountants know this and they price every project in advance and notify the client at the outset the scope and the price of the project.

Doesn't visit or call me vs. Visits and calls on a systematic basis.

Your clients are not Accountants. Your clients are typically business-people. We know how to run our business. We know how to make our product, sell our product and service our product. We do not understand all the 'ebbs and flows' of cashflow. And we're so busy doing what we do that we do not call you. Most people think you charge for every phone call so we don't call or communicate nearly as much as we should. What if you called us and visited us from time to time. I remember

> Quotable quote:
>
> "I would love it if (Partner name) would call me up from time to time and simply ask 'how's it going'?"

vividly I was running a 'Client Advisory Board' meeting for a firm in regional New Zealand. The partners were not in the room and I was interviewing 10 of the firm's best clients in a group meeting. I asked the question 'what else could your Accountant do for you?' A paint retailer called Barry said, "I would love it if (Partner name) would call me up from time to time and simply ask 'how's it going?'". Simple stuff. Yet so powerful. If you did call and visit your clients on a systematic basis then they will love you for it and you will pick up a lot more work. Real Time Accountants know this and are doing it.

Doesn't follow up vs. Follows up on every opportunity.

It has been a pleasure serving the Accounting profession since 1994. There are so many positives that I continue inventing, re-inventing and offering new methods and ideas. One thing that does annoy me a lot is that most Accountants do not follow up on opportunities. They may get a lead or an enquiry or even run a seminar and have people wanting to buy. Yet they do not follow up. I am not sure why (maybe they think it's too tacky) they don't follow up. In this day and age you cannot wait any longer. You need to create opportunity and then follow up on them. Real Time Accountants have a special nose on them. They can sniff out opportunities and they know how to follow up on them.

Doesn't promote the latest thing vs. Always promoting.

The ultimate goal for an Accounting firm is to have every client buying every service they need to achieve their goals. If that is the case then Real Time Accountants are constantly on the lookout for the next idea/method/product that will help their clients. Sadly Redundant Data Accountants are not on the lookout for the latest thing. They are happy to sit in their office, go to technical tax sessions to get their 'CPE' hours or do nothing. Same old. Same old. The Real Time Accountants are constantly attending different types of workshops and seminars. They are reading all of the time. They are networking and they have a thirst for learning. They don't see the service or the idea they are promoting to their clients as selling. They see it as servicing. They are always promoting something to their client that helps them achieve their goals.

Most clients on a 'hard drive' accounting system vs. Most clients on 'cloud' accounting.

It is almost impossible to be a Real Time Accountant if your client's accounting system is on a hard drive rather than the Internet – aka the cloud. The minute the client saves the Accounting data to the USB stick or emails it to you it is out of date. You will always be a Redundant Data Accountant when the accounting system is not on the Internet. With Internet-based accounting technology you truly can be real time. You have access to the data as it is happening at the client site. You can

> Quotable quote:
>
> *"The minute the client saves the Accounting data to the USB stick or emails it to you it is out of date."*

predict what is going to happen as the trend lines appear. You can advise your client based on real time data. The Real Time Accountants are promoting cloud accounting heavily to their clients. Their future relies on it.

Numbers power with the client vs. Numbers power with the Accountant.

Back in the day (whenever that was) your clients used to bring in their financial information for you to interpret, prepare, manipulate and file. They would physically bring in bank statements, invoices, receipts, inventory lists, contracts, equipment details and so on. You would then prepare the accounting information based on the data presented. You would then present the financial information back to them and tell them their profit, revenue and other key numbers. The numbers power used to rest with the Accountant. These days the accounting software applications are so powerful that reports are generated with a click of a button (we used to buy those from you) and the analysis is so rich that I can make management decisions based on what a software application tells me. The numbers power is now with the client. The Real Time Accountants

> Quotable quote:
>
> *"The Real Time Accountants are bringing the numbers power back to them."*

are bringing the numbers power back to them. They are formally connecting their clients to them through software (not Accounting software but business advisory software) like **www.panalitix.com** and they are monitoring the performance in real time. It's time to bring the numbers power back to the Accountant.

In 2014 we surveyed 428 business owners on what they wanted from their Accountant. One of the questions was about the type of Accountant you would like to work with – A Redundant data Accountants or Real Time Accountant. An explanation was given and as you can see by the table, an overwhelming 93% said they wanted a Real Time Accountant.

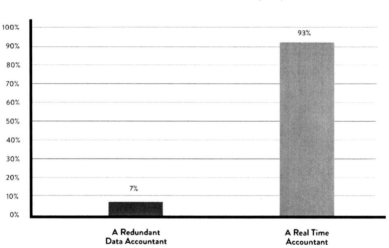

What sort of accountant would you prefer?

It's your choice to become a Real Time Accountant or remain a Redundant Data Accountant. The future of the profession is Real Time! I hope you choose to be one.

What clients really want

There are 2 schools of thought on finding out what a customer wants and what they are prepared to pay for.

The first I'll call the Henry Ford way. Mr. Ford (who founded the Ford Motor Company) famously said that if he asked his customers what they wanted they would have said '*a faster horse*.' He didn't ask his customers what they wanted instead he designed something that they needed. However, the customer didn't know that they needed it yet.

A modern example is the late Steve Jobs who co-founded Apple. Mr. Jobs didn't ask us if we thought having 'a thousand songs in our pocket'

was a good idea. He built the iPod®
anyway. He didn't ask us if we thought
blending music, phone, calendar,
Internet, navigation and so on into one
device was a good idea. He built the
iPhone® anyway. He didn't ask us if
we wanted to carry around yet another
device so we could consume content
and do quick work on the fly. He built

> Quotable quote:
>
> *"Many hundreds of billions of dollars in sales later would indicate we liked his company's inventions."*

the iPad® anyway. Many hundreds of billions of dollars in sales later
would indicate we liked his company's inventions.

So the first way is to be an extraordinary visionary and tell the marketplace
what they need. Then create services and
products that don't exist yet. Educate
the market why they need this new cool
thing and hope like crazy that they buy
it. You have to back yourself!

> Quotable quote:
>
> *"Educate the market why they need this new cool thing and hope like crazy that they buy it. You have to back yourself!"*

The second way is to ask. Seeing how
most Accountants are not visionaries
then this is probably a safer option.

Asking can take many formats. You could send out a survey. You
could run a client advisory board where you have 8-10 of your best
clients in a room and an independent facilitator asks what they like,
don't like and what they would like to see improved or added if they
were the owners. You could ask every client 1-on-1 at a 'coffee' meeting.

Or you could do all 3.

Whichever way you ask you have to be prepared for the brutal truth
coming out. You have to be prepared to take action and make some
changes. You have to listen.

Many years ago I was facilitating a series of 3 client advisory boards
for the new owner of a company he just bought.. I arranged 30 of the best
clients into 3 separate meetings. Some of the clients traveled a long way
to get to the meeting and they were honored to be invited to give their
candid feedback. The feedback from the first meeting was amazing. The
clients told us many insights for improvement, innovation and service.

It was fabulous. On the way to the restaurant the new owner said to me, *'What did you think of that?'* I told him I thought it was brilliant feedback and many of it we should act on. He said *'they have no (insert expletive here) idea what they are talking about.'* I was gob smacked. The next 2 meetings he did not give the clients a chance to speak.

> Quotable quote:
>
> *"He said 'they have no (insert expletive here) idea what they are talking about.' I was gob smacked."*

He simply told them what he was going to do with his new company. They didn't like it. He made the changes anyway without feedback. The business went from $25M in revenue to a disastrous $5M in revenue in 12 months flat.

To help you out my company did a bit of asking for you. We had 50 or so Accountants send out a survey request to their clients. We so had a cross section of firms and 428 business clients responded. It was all anonymous and the results tell the story.

One of the early set of questions was around communication. We were specifically looking for how well Accountants communicate now and what their clients want. With face-to-face communication you can see by the table below that 62% want more face-to-face contact. Of course, provided there is value in the meeting.

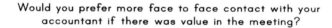

Would you prefer more face to face contact with your accountant if there was value in the meeting?

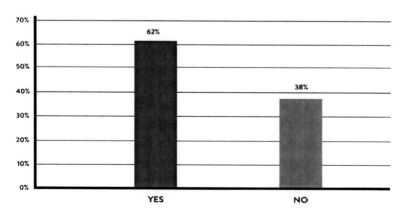

The key is that there is value in the meeting. You are busy and your clients are busy. If there is value then (judging by 428 responses) your clients are receptive to meeting you more frequently. To create value why don't you do a brainstorm meeting in your office on the client. Come up with some ideas for improvement and take those ideas to the client.

> Quotable quote:
> *"To create value why don't you do a brainstorm meeting in your office on the client."*

Face-to-face meetings take time. A phone call does not. A touch base 'how's it going call' is seriously valuable and shows that you are interested in their affairs. As you can see below a staggering 40% of clients NEVER get a call from their Accountant. What a wasted opportunity to add value and maybe find a new project. More than half got a call never or once per year.

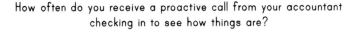

How often do you receive a proactive call from your accountant checking in to see how things are?

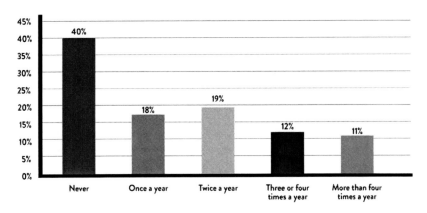

I ask Accountants all the time if they have good relationships with their clients. An overwhelming YES is the response. To create a relationship it requires communication. How can you honestly have a good relationship with someone if you only meet with them 1-2 times per year and speak with them once per year? Just imagine if you only spoke to your life partner (assuming you have one) at home once or twice a year. How would the relationship be? For some of you… better!

So how much communication is too much? Just by asking the target market some still say (12%) that they do not want any phone communication from you. It's interesting that 40% do not get a call now yet 12% do not want a call.

> Quotable quote:
>
> *"How can you honestly have a good relationship with someone if you only meet with them 1-2 times per year and speak with them once per year?"*

So I am thinking thinking that 28% of the '*I don't get a call now*' group do actually want a call. The vast majority in our survey (78%) think a proactive call anything from 1 to 4 times per year would be a good idea. So call it 2 or 3 times per year.

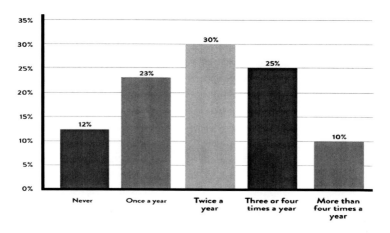

How often would you like to be proactively called (for free) by your accountant checking in to see how things are going?

This is not rocket science. The service levels are so bad in the Accounting profession that anything simple like a proactive phone call to 'check in' can make the world of difference to the perception of you, your business and your services.

Our research indicates a client will leave an Accountant for either 'Service' or 'Services.' They are either unhappy with the customer service (speed of communication, turnaround time, etc) or with the services they are buying or not buying from you. Under the services banner it includes value for money, pricing, mistakes or something else they think they need but are not getting.

We asked the 428 business owners 'if you had to choose one thing, what should your Accountant do?' We gave them 5 possible answers.

1. Do more marketing
2. Lift your service levels
3. Be more transperant with your pricing
4. Focus more on the future rather than the past
5. Offer more services that help me improve my business

If we bunch no. 2 and 3 together (service levels and pricing) then we get 31%. I am going to call those the 'Service' answers. If we bunch 3 & 4 together (better advice and valuable services) we get 61%. This would be the 'Services' answers. A staggering 92% said that they want more from you and they want you to improve your customer service.

If you had to choose one of the following pieces of advice to assist your accountant, which would you choose?

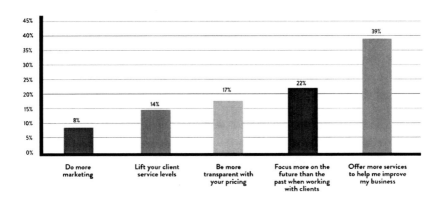

The business community has spoken loud and clear. Your clients want more help, more communication and better customer service. I know you're busy (doing compliance) and that can no longer be an excuse. We're all busy and time allocation is a priority not a resource.

You must get a systematic program in place for contacting your clients. You must offer more services that really help your clients' financial condition.

> Quotable quote:
>
> *"You have financial intimacy right now with your clients. That's why they stay with you."*

You have financial intimacy right now with your clients. That's why they stay with you. You know things about them that very few people do. If you want to keep them then you need to increase the level of financial intimacy. You need to improve the customer service and you need to broaden your service offering. Since I started in this profession in 1994 I have been saying the same thing in many different ways. Be proactive and add value. If you don't, someone else will.

Technology makes it too easy

Accountants have been in the 'pursuit of efficiency' for as long as I can remember. You have electronic working papers, e-mail, document management, knowledge management, social media, 2 and 3 screens on every desk, intranets, portals, cloud accounting for your clients and super-fast computers! The list goes on and on.

It's a never-ending quest to get the work done efficiently and accurately. But at what cost? Because of the quest to drive efficiencies you seem to have dropped the ball in 2 areas:

> Quotable quote:
>
> *"It's a never-ending quest to get the work done efficiently and accurately. But at what cost?"*

1. Team members no longer think about the client situation
2. There is less real communication with your clients

I think the technology is 'dumbing down' the value of the Accountant. Before technology Accountants had to think about the client's situation more and communicate (with spoken words) more than they do now. These days the Accountant just needs to know which keys to hit in which order on the keyboard.

It seems Accountants would rather 'rip off an email' and think their job is done rather than give the client a call. It seems Accountants would rather send work via email or courier rather than present the work to the client. I think most of the value created is in the conversation and the presentation.

Take a look at what the 428 business owners told us when it comes to annual accounts. Over half (52%) said they got their year-end work either emailed, posted or couriered to them for signing.

This is disgraceful. Most of the profession's revenue is in compliance right now. This is your primary product and you email it to your clients for signing! Save me please. No wonder clients do not value compliance! You don't value it. You downplay the value of it by emailing it. I (and your clients) have 2 primary questions when it comes to our year end financials.

1. How much tax do I have to pay and why?
2. Where did the money go?

How will I know those answers if you email me your primary product? I do also wonder what happens in the face-to-face (45% of occasions) meetings. I bet they are not structured nor do they offer a huge amount of value.

Stop sending your primary product for signing via courier post or email. You are wasting an opportunity to add value, ask questions and maybe find another project.

> Quotable quote:
>
> *"Stop sending your primary product for signing via courier post or email."*

Make sure when you do meet with your client to present the year end accounts that you actually explain what they mean. Make sure you do a 3-year historical 'Business Performance Review' at least once per year to add value to the history. Make sure that you ask (in this meeting) what their goals are and then you can start to match services that help them achieve their goals.

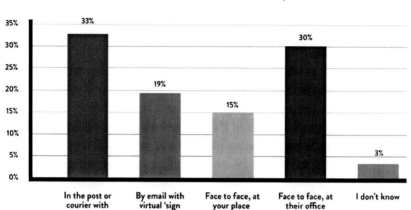

How does your accountant present your year end financial statements and tax returns to you?

Technology can certainly make our lives easier and more efficient. Technology should enhance a client experience not diminish it.

> **Quotable quote:**
>
> *"Without a doubt the no. 1 technology thing that you can do in your firm is to suggest/encourage/cajole/insist your clients move to a cloud accounting product."*

Without a doubt the no. 1 technology thing that you can do in your firm is to suggest/encourage/cajole/insist your clients move to a cloud accounting product. Although there are issues (outlined in my Dear Accountant letter and Chapter 1 about the dinosaurs) associated with cloud accounting I think it is the most important thing you can do with your clients. The issues are only issues if you do nothing about the efficiency gains you get from using cloud based accounting.

With your clients on a desktop product you have redundant data. With your clients on cloud accounting you can be so much more real time. You can add value now, not later. You can get a heartbeat of your clients every day. You

> **Quotable quote:**
>
> *"With your clients on cloud accounting you can be so much more real time."*

can make a massive difference to their financial condition. You can take the 'financial intimacy' up a number of levels.

Many firms are insisting that 100% of their clients move across to a cloud based accounting system. It just makes sense to do so. The vast majority of firms will have 2-3 products in their client base. Most Accountants will not align themselves with just one provider. I think that is the right thing to do. You match the product to the clients' needs.

There are many firms who are going further than just promoting a cloud based accounting system. The ultimate solution at the client's site is where every aspect of the technology 'talks' to each other. The accounting data is integrated with the customer data. The accounting and customer data is integrated with the inventory control data and all that integrates with the distribution system. So the entire supply chain is covered. All of that data is consolidated into daily 'dashboards' so the business owners can see what is going on in every aspect of their business. This sort of technology used to cost millions of dollars to buy and implement. Because of the massive development in cloud computing you can get it for a few hundred dollars per month.

The right technology can give the business owner better data to make better management decisions. You can be at the center of all the technology by recommending systems which will help.

You are the expert in financial coaching. With better data you can be a better financial coach. With the right technology and the right data you truly can become the Real Time Accountant.

What to do with the data

As you become the Real Time Accountant one of the key steps is to strongly recommend that your clients migrate across to a cloud accounting solution. That'll take 12 - 36 months to systematically help your clients change. Let's assume you have done that. You have spent the time training them. You have helped them to get good data in, so good data can come out. You have got them actively checking their financial situation on a more regular basis. Your clients love the new reporting and they are able to make better management decisions.

What about you? You used to sell management reporting now the computer is doing it for free.

As I have said a number of times so far with cloud accounting implemented with your clients, you now have access to more 'real time' financial data than ever before. With the data being so up to date there is an amazing opportunity for you to add value with new services.

You can even take it up a notch and get daily and automatic 'KPI feeds' direct to your device (web browser and/or email) that will tell you the story as to what is going on – good and bad. We asked the 428 business owners if they were interested in you having direct access to their data in real time and then send you alerts and advice if something untoward is happening. As you can see 21% are not interested at all yet 79% said they were interested in this, said it was worth exploring or suggested that is what you should be doing in the first place!

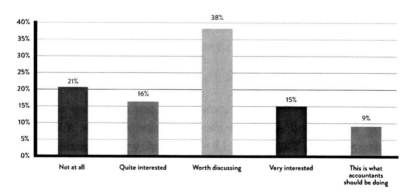

If your accountant had access to technology that would enable them to keep an eye on your financials and key performance indicators in real time, then send you alerts and advice if something is going off track, assuming this was priced reasonably; how interested would would you be in pursuing it?

With real time data consolidated into one location using tools like PANALITIX (**www.panalitix.com**) you can interpret the numbers, be alerted to what is going on and then advise your clients accordingly.

With all of this data at your fingertips, what are you going to do with it? I think you have a duty of care and obligation to advise the clients how to improve the numbers. If you are living by the mantra of *all clients are buying all services that help them achieve their goals* then it's not selling new services. It's servicing your clients properly.

Here is a list of 14 services that you could offer:

> Quotable quote:
>
> *"If you are living by the mantra of 'all clients are buying all services that help them achieve their goals' then it's not selling new services."*

1. Cash flow forecasting and analysis
2. Profit improvement program
3. Monitoring & accountability program
4. Debt re-structuring
5. Capital raising
6. Interest reduction service
7. Waste audit
8. Revenue improvement strategies
9. Creditor analysis & negotiation
10. Product profitability analysis
11. Debtor management service
12. Tax planning & tax minimization
13. Business Planning
14. Inventory management system

All are valuable services that will make a significant impact to your client's financial future. By 'staying close to the numbers' you have a better chance of the client buying the service. With good systemization of the services you can have Accountants of all levels deliver the service – not just the Partners.

You will need to learn some sales skills on how to have your clients buy them. You will also need some new tools (get rid of the spreadsheets, please) so you can systemize the services. Now here's the big one. We all know that cashflow (lack thereof) is the main reason businesses fail. The number one issue in businesses around the world right now is cashflow management.

We all know it and the Accounting profession is uniquely placed to help improve it.

Your clients want it as well. Well, not all clients want it. In our survey 29% said they did not. However, 71% said that if the service was reasonably priced and they could see value in it then they would be interested in exploring the idea.

If your Accountant could offer a cash flow monitoring service, including an annual budget and cash flow forecast, a monthly report, an annual meeting, proactive alerts and advice and ad hoc phone access, assuming this was priced reasonably, how interested would you be in pursuing it?

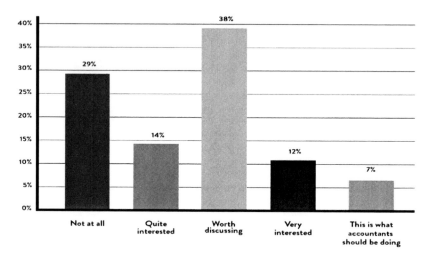

It's a no brainer. I ask Accountants what's the most valuable service they can offer to their business clients. No surprises. It is cashflow monitoring and forecasting. So if it's the most valuable then how many of your business clients have a live, working, accurate and real time cashflow forecast? Very few is always

> Quotable quote:
>
> *"We want to know how much free cash we have each month to spend on whatever we want to spend it on."*

the answer. Yet this is the most valuable thing you can do. Here's what we (the business community) want when it comes to cashflow. We want to know how much free cash we have each month to spend on whatever we want to spend it on. We want to know how we are tracking and what we can do to improve it. Your clients are not financial analysts like you. You can help us in this area.

The service you provide is a cashflow forecasting and monitoring service. In your definition you call it a '3 way rolling cashflow.' It covers the cashflow forecast, the profit and loss and the balance sheet. If your client is borrowing money from a bank then the bank wants it. Even if your client is not borrowing money then it is a good thing to have. The problem with 'hard drive' based systems (or heaven forbid spreadsheets) is that once they are created they are out of date. By using old technology you cannot monitor the cashflow unless it is manually entered.

With cloud accounting and 'add on' partners like PANALITIX you can do this automatically. You can prepare the forecast based on historical data plus some planning. You can 'normalize' the numbers month to month with the client. You can consolidate the data as it is transacted at the client's end and because the accounting data is linked to the 'bank feeds', the cashflow, the forecast and the balance sheet is kept up to date every single day. Now that's Real Time Accounting!

If the bank needs an update then you can provide it quickly. If your client wants it then you can provide it quickly. If you have got your client on a monitoring service then you can be immensely valuable.

Becoming the Real Time Accountant is more than a goal, a wish, a hope or a mindset shift. It's about changing your behavior, your systems, your technology and your services. It's about making a difference.

RIP the Redundant Data Accountant. **Rise...the Real Time Accountant.**

Chapter 4
People are still needed

The current team may be short lived

Around the world technology is disrupting many jobs in many industries. Among jobs in the firing line include those that involve repetition, problem solving, information dissemination and data processing. If there is any type of human algorithm involved it can now be done by a computer or a robot. If there is manual data entry then much of that can be done by supercomputers with barcoding. If there is consistent repetition in the job in the future it can be done by software and supercomputers. If there is information dissemination involved then that can be done by the Internet and clever algorithms.

Sound like anyone we know? Yes – you!

The current team members might be short lived if technology takes hold the way I think it will. Due to technology there has been significant progress in how clients interact with their Accountants.

Here is a rudimentary summary of how a client interacts with their Accountant:

1. Client has problem / opportunity or requirement to interact with an Accountant
2. Client contacts Accountant (or vice versa) and Accountant tells client what information is required
3. Client sends in relevant information
4. Accountant checks that information is complete
5. Accountant processes the information

6. Accountant creates report/letter/study/meeting/structure and presents to client
7. Accountant lodges/files the information with relevant parties
8. Client says well done & pays the bill

It's been the same process since from before the days that Accountants have been tracking time!

What's changed? The only thing that has changed are the technology and tools so the job could be done more efficiently. Here is a timeline of technology usage in Accounting firms over the years:

➢ Paper receipts were delivered by horse in an old shoe box
➢ Paper receipts were entered into a handwritten cashbook
➢ Handwritten equations and a lot of thinking worked out the client's situation
➢ The postal service enabled distribution of information
➢ The handwritten cashbook was turned into a spreadsheet
➢ There was 1 computer in the office and it had its own charge code
➢ The spreadsheet was saved to a floppy disk
➢ There was a paper based 'working paper' and paper filing in big filing cabinets
➢ A calculator replaced the pencil and paper equation
➢ There was a thing called a fax machine and clients faxed in information
➢ The spreadsheet turned into software and it was saved to a floppy disk
➢ There was a pool of computers in the office administered by experts
➢ The software on a floppy disk got too big so it was saved to a CD-ROM
➢ The firm had one email address only and a slow (dial up) Internet connection
➢ The software on the CD-ROM got too big so it was saved to a USB stick
➢ There was computer on every desk with one screen
➢ Electronic work papers appeared and paper filing still existed

➢ Scanners started appearing on each Accountant's desk
➢ Everyone had an email address and they now had 2 computer screens per person
➢ The paperless office is now a reality
➢ The Internet speed increased dramatically
➢ Powerful searching could now take place on the Internet – no need for books
➢ Accountants started to get 3 screens on every desk
➢ Accountants got very good at using the software in front of them
➢ Cloud-based software appeared and the Accountants' world changed forever!
➢ Any of this bringing back memories?

> Quotable quote:
>
> *"What's happened with all this technology? I think it has 'dumbed down' the value of an Accountant."*

What's happened with all this technology? I think it has 'dumbed down' the value of an Accountant. These days Accountants need to know which keys (on the keyboard) to hit in which order and how to use the software. What happened to the thinking behind Accounting? I think the thinking has gone. The technology has taken away the smarts of an Accountant.

Cloud based accounting software has found its feet and by the year 2020 it will be commonplace in the majority of small to medium businesses. Because the cloud based accounting software is driven by very smart supercomputers, the Accountants that we have today are not needed. You can get computing power to do most of that work. There's an app for that!

What the industry needs is the Accountant of yesteryear. **Before technology the 'yesteryear Accountant'** used basic technology like a pencil and paper to solve client problems. They had to think about what was going on and manually work it out. They gave real advice based on wisdom and experience.

These days the computer is working out the clients' problems and the Internet is giving the advice. Soon it will all blend into one and the 'App' will work it out and give the advice. If you have an iPhone® think

Siri for business.

To Remain Relevant the Accountant must add value to what is in front of them. If you don't (as explained in Chapter 1) you may go the way of the dinosaur. I am not saying that Accountants will be 100% redundant. Not at all. I think a whole new market can be created by Accountants where the industry looks nothing like what it does today.

> Quotable quote:
>
> *"I think a whole new market can be created by Accountants where the industry looks nothing like what it does today."*

That new market is where the entire industry is giving an experience to the human that the computer cannot. That new market is financial coaching, business counselling & business advisory.

We'll still need people in the industry but not as many 'Redundant Data Accountants.' If that's you then get out now or change.

A virtual team

In 2014 there were approximately 50,000 Australian office jobs sent to the Philippines alone. According to experts this number is set to double this year and continue growing each year. It can be a touchy subject with some people but it's not going to go away. Clothing has been manufactured overseas for years and now it's office jobs. When the labor costs are $1/5^{th}$ to $1/10^{th}$ of what we pay in Western countries it is a compelling opportunity for businesses to consider. There is also an abundance of people who are educated and very keen to work.

Although many Asian countries are offering outsourcing resources, I am most familiar with the Philippines market. There are approximately 1.2M people currently hired (in the offshoring/ outsourcing space) and it is growing at 20% pa. They cannot build the office facilities fast enough to house them all. To become a qualified CPA it takes 5 years after university and you can hire them for around $4 - $7 per hour. This is considered a good salary.

> Quotable quote:
>
> *"To become a qualified CPA it takes 5 years after university and you can hire them for around $4 - $7 per hour."*

When I first visited on an outsourcing study tour the following line got me: "*any job that is done over the phone or behind a computer we can do for a 1/5th to a 1/10th of the cost.*" So basically any non-customer facing role can be done cheaper and often better.

The use of cloud technology is critical to making this happen in accounting firms. Instead of sending large data files backwards and forwards, the offshore Accountants are working on the same file you are. If Accountants locally are not adding value to the work they are doing then their days are numbered.

The Accounting firm of the future will have local team members who are customer facing and adding value. Everything else will be done somewhere else. This is happening right now.

Many Accountants I have spoken with reject this reality because they still want to hire 'locally.' Hiring local people is a very noble thing to do. I do it but I do it for customer facing roles mainly. Many Accountants are worried what will happen to the profession if they don't hire local graduates and train them. This is a good concern to have. It's also a real one. If you are going to shift your processing team offshore then how are you going to train local talent to 'come through the ranks'? The entire training model might need to be turned on its head as well.

The challenge you have got is other firms are doing this and they are using the significant cost savings as an advantage and they are reducing their prices. With an (up to) 80% cost reduction on labor costs the ones that are using offshore teams can hire more people and give a better service. They can do more marketing, create more products and give a better experience to their clients.

> Quotable quote:
>
> "With an (up to) 80% cost reduction on labor costs the ones that are using offshore teams can hire more people and give a better service."

The biggest challenge you will have with this strategy is 'selling it' to your existing team members. They will feel their jobs are threatened. If you take the view it is a business growth strategy and not a redundancy strategy then that will help a lot.

You don't have to go in 'boots 'n all' and create your own full-time team from day one. You could start by hiring contractors on the various contractor websites to do one-off special projects.

In the not too distant future here's what your offshore team could look like:

- ✓ Administration
- ✓ Your internal finance team
- ✓ Marketing team – all functions
- ✓ Sales coordinators
- ✓ Client services assistants
- ✓ Technology creation and support
- ✓ Accounting processing team
- ✓ Bookkeepers
- ✓ Para-planners
- ✓ Product & systems developers

If you are interested in this space then I strongly suggest you hop on a plane and go on a study tour (email me and I'll send you details of reputable tour operators) so you can see it for yourself. As the tour operator (Mike) said to me:

'Many people come over here with their current business or product in mind. Then they see the machine in action. When they leave they have invented new businesses and new product ideas'.

The machine is full of gas and is waiting to be started.

> Quotable quote:
> "Many people come over here with their current business or product in mind. Then they see the machine in action. When they leave they have invented new businesses and new product ideas."

Team engagement

It's hard to grow and develop an Accounting firm on your own. You need the support of your team. You may want to implement a lot of the ideas from this book however your team may have other ideas. Unless you have a super flexible team who is used to change then

> Quotable quote:
> "Unless you have a super flexible team who is used to change then the reality is you may struggle with team engagement or buy in."

the reality is you may struggle with team engagement or buy in. You may struggle to get the change you're looking for.

Everything in this book is about change management. It's all about doing something different to get a different result. With that comes behavior challenges. If someone has been successfully (in their eyes) doing the same thing for 15 or 20 years and all of a sudden you want them to take a sharp right turn and do something different sometimes they resist.

Team engagement is not a singular event. It seems some Partners think that sending the team to a seminar will do the trick. They'll get all enthused, learn some new skills and hey presto it all changes. Sadly this is not the case. Team engagement is a process.

In my last book '*Accounting Practices Don't Add Up*' I dedicated a whole chapter on building a high performing team and there was some excellent work (according to readers) on team engagement and buy in. Here is an updated 8 point summary:

1. **Vision.** For a team to be on the same page there first must be a page to be on. Do you have a one-page plan (not a lengthy business plan) and a painted picture of your vision? Do you know what it looks like when it is done? Does the team?

2. **Leadership.** If you settle on an idea / plan / strategy / process then the leadership team must practice what they preach. So many times I hear of well-intentioned plans go astray because one of the leadership team members went back to their old ways.

3. **Culture standards.** Have you documented your culture so everyone knows how they are to behave whilst interacting with each other? Every firm I meet wants to improve the culture. What does an improved culture look like? Send me an email and I'll send you some examples.

4. **Quarterly Themes.** These really rock! You work out your biggest challenge or opportunity for the quarter and you wrap a theme around it. You dress the office up. You get everyone involved and have fun with it. Some examples might be 'home run', 'buzz', 'round up', 'growing the grass' and 'delivering happiness'. Each quarterly theme has a daily metric that you can measure and track progress.

Like the number of clients, number of new opportunities, number of testimonials, etc.

5. **Meetings.** More meetings and less time per meeting is the mantra. Make them short, stand up and directive. Make them regular with no waffle (give me the baby not the delivery) and make them at odd times like 0747, 0808, 1010, 1251. Only 3 questions 1) What's up today? 2) What's your daily metric? 3) Where are you stuck?

> Quotable quote:
>
> *"More meetings and less time per meeting is the mantra. Make them short, stand up and directive."*

6. **Reporting systems.** Why do Accountants hide the profit, the cash flow and the revenue? Remember that your team are Accountants and they can probably work it out. What's there to hide anyway? If you let the team know of the KPI's and the results of those KPI's then you've got a better than good chance of achieving the results. It's a popular management technique called 'open book management.'

7. **Daily sprints.** Sitting behind a keyboard all day with limited human interaction can be a bit boring. Why not have some fun and create a competitive spirit every day. You could introduce the concept of 'sprints' where there are daily prizes for the activities done. The first person to get a completed project out the door gets $10. The first person to find another project within a project gets a voucher of some sort. Mix it up and have fun and you'll be amazed the buzz that you'll create.

8. **Accountability.** How often do you 'call people' on their commitments? How often do you publicly remind people of what they committed to? You said you would do it – why didn't you? You don't have to say much to hold people accountable. Being embarrassed in front of their peers is often enough. Someone once said to me *'if you want someone to be accountable they*

> Quotable quote:
>
> *"If you want someone to be accountable they must be in control of that they are accountable to."*

must be in control of that they are accountable to.' It's great to hold people accountable to their actions but they need to be able to implement. They need to be in control of whatever they are accountable to.

If all this fails then the last resort is to *'coach then fire.'* What do you do if the plan is solid, the explanation of the change is articulated well, the Partners endorse it, regular coaching and training has happened and they still don't get it? Simple...

Fire them.

Free up their future and let them go and work at another traditional Accounting firm. Let them go and ruin someone else's firm. Sometimes you have to take a hard line and put F.I.F.O. in place. Fit In or F#@% Off!

Rewarding your team

I have a view that for a fair days work a fair day's salary should be given. I do not believe you should overpay people (base salary) just to keep them or get them in the first place. If you create a great culture where people are challenged, they are learning a lot and they are having fun then they will stay with you regardless (within reason) of the base salary.

> Quotable quote:
>
> *"I do not believe you should overpay people (base salary) just to keep them or get them in the first place."*

Rewards come in many formats.

On the first day (or as close to it) of a new team member starting I have 5 minutes with them. They have already been through many hoops just to get a job and they are now in the induction process. They have been allocated to a team and they typically report to someone else other than me. They are sometimes a bit nervous for that first week as they are settling in. Here's how my very important speech goes.

I call it the Leaving Speech.

"[insert newbie name here], welcome to the team. We're thrilled you're here. I am sure you're the right person for the job and I know there is a lot going on this week. I just wanted to talk to you for a few minutes about the day you leave. You will leave one day, everyone does. I know this is your first day and I know you'll leave sometime in the future so I figured we should talk about it now. I have a number of hopes and desires for that inevitable day. Firstly, I hope we part on good terms. I don't want someone to fire you because you didn't work out or make you redundant because of a business downturn. Secondly, I hope that you learn a lot, contribute a lot and have a lot of fun. Thirdly, I hope that you live by our values, service and culture standards and the standards we set become part of your life. And lastly when you look back at this block of time, no matter how long it is, you look back on it fondly as an amazing part of your career. Welcome to the team. That's all I wanted to say."

It's an interesting meeting to have because who gets to talk about leaving the business they just started. Often they gasp and look at me weird. I like to think it sets the scene for the future. Learn a lot, contribute a lot, have fun, live by our values and standards and look at this time fondly as an important time in your career. To give the gift of learning, contributing, having fun, and giving great service is an awesome reward.

I think a reward is having a snappy office environment. Most places you go to are not that nice and your team is going to spend 40+ hours a week in this location. It needs to be uplifting and inspiring. I think the reward of recognition is a powerful one. To recognize people publicly for a job well done is a very powerful motivator. A clap, a mention or a card goes a long way.

> Quotable quote:
> *"To recognize people publicly for a job well done is a very powerful motivator. A clap, a mention or a card goes a long way."*

I think the reward of positivity and laughter in the office is very powerful. The team members' home life may not be that great but when they come to work they enjoy themselves. The reward of formal learning with a 'book of the month' program or many seminars is both helpful and useful. It is amazing to see how a team will pull together to reach a target when a day off or a week of extra leave is offered. Team dinners and dress up occasions are always fun and add to the culture.

I once encouraged my team into writing their personal goals down at an annual business planning session. I provided inspirational magazines, special writing paper and a motivating environment. They were charged with writing 100+ life goals in a 2 hour timeframe. Most did. When they finished the exercise I collected the papers, made a copy and told them I wanted to help them achieve their goals. The goals went into my safe at home. What they didn't know was I went through the goals and bought something special for each person for that upcoming Christmas. It was a magical Christmas party with my 'Santa sack' full of goodies that they all wanted. We had tears, laughter and excitement as Santa handed out the gifts. Then we all got very drunk!

After much debate and researching I have worked out that profit share systems and commissions do not work for anyone else other than salespeople.

It's not about the money. The money is important but it's more than that. It's about the experience.

> Quotable quote:
>
> *"After much debate and researching I have worked out that profit share systems and commissions do not work for anyone else other than salespeople."*

Chapter 5
Over-delivering on service

Communicating until it hurts

If a client pays you a high fee do you communicate with them more? Absolutely you say. Should you wait for them to pay you more before you communicate with them? Or should you communicate with them more before they pay you more? I think the latter should apply.

If you increase the level of communication then you'll increase the level of trust. If you increase the level of trust you'll increase the level of relationship. If you increase the level of relationship you'll increase the level of fee per client. If you increase the level of fee per client you'll increase the referral rate. If you increase the referral rate you'll increase the happiness level. If you increase the happiness level then everything is sorted!

> Quotable quote:
> *"If you increase the level of relationship you'll increase the level of fee per client."*

It all starts with increasing the level of communication. How much communication and in what format is the key. After years working with Accounting firms and their clients I have worked out that the diagram below is the ultimate communication schedule. It should be applied to all clients you want to keep.

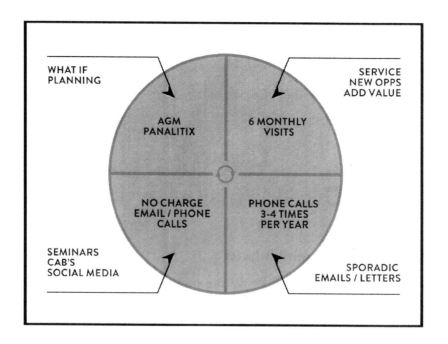

There are 4 parts to this schedule.

1. An annual general meeting
2. Visits to see how they are going
3. Phone calls and sporadic communication
4. Not charging for 'attendance' communication

The Annual General Meeting

Every year you finalize the annual accounts for your client. What is your process at this point? Is it all of those inane 'sign here' stickers with little or no explanation? Do you send out the draft accounts for signing?

My guess is that the majority of your clients get a substandard explanation of the previous year's financial performance. As a business client I have 2 main questions at year end: 1) How much tax do I have to pay and why? and 2) Where did the money go?

If you are glossing over this then you are missing out on loads of opportunities. You are missing out on great customer service and potential revenue opportunities for you. I recommend that you have an AGM process. This happens once per year. Of course all of the signing needs to take place but more importantly explanation needs to take place.

When it comes to #clientsunderstandingwhatyouhavedone typically the reports that come out of your tax preparation software is not that great. If you just send it to us then we don't understand it. It's full of numbers and words that confuse us.

The Accountants that we work with are using a different process. They are adding a 'Business Performance Review' which is a 3 year historical review of the clients' financial affairs in one easy-to-view screen. They are using our PANALITIX (**www.panalitix.com**) software to do this. The Business Performance Review is a conversation starter. It shows trends, issues and opportunities in critical areas of a business. It is designed to be simple so the clients can see what is going on. It is presented on a screen (the bigger the better) and of course you can print it out. You can do some financial modeling and 'what if' based analysis. It typically results in the clients saying 'how do we fix it' – or words to that effect.

The objective of this meeting is to understand their current situation fully (by knowing the numbers and asking questions), understand their objectives going forward (by asking questions) and having a discussion how you can help them get there.

This AGM meeting should be conducted with every business client you want to keep. Never charge for this meeting. It's on you and it's a value adding opportunity, plus who knows, you might win some more business from it. As a minimum you'll give some great customer service.

Client visits

All clients love it when you visit them at their place of business. Most do not do it enough and some Accountants do not do it at all. If you don't do it you are missing out on massive opportunities to add value and create new business from existing clients. I used to call this meeting a 'nurturing' visit. A few years back I changed the terminology to a sales visit.

The purpose of the meeting is to understand your clients' current situation more, understand their short and long term objectives and to see if you can help them achieve their objectives. It's a sales meeting. As a sales meeting you do not want to leave anything to chance. You need a systematic approach to the meeting so you can get a predictable outcome.

This is the only part I have replicated from my first book 'Accounting Practices Don't Add Up'. I felt it was that important to reiterate again. It's my 12-step meeting approach:

Step 1.   Make sure all of the decision-makers are at the meeting

Step 2.   Set the scene why we are having the meeting – the client is wondering

Step 3.   Frame the meeting's purpose and time frame of the meeting

Step 4.   Understand the 'now' by asking a series of background related questions

Step 5.   Understand what the clients' goals and objectives are – what they want to achieve

Step 6.   Ask how they would know if they have achieved their objectives

Step 7.   Ask what it would mean to them if we helped them achieve their objectives

Step 8.   Ask what their current plans are to achieve their objectives

Step 9.   Ask what the consequences are of not doing something different

Step 10. Ask timing related questions – when they want to get started to achieve their objectives

Step 11. Tell the client the next steps – write a plan to achieve objectives with options to take

Step 12. Book the next steps – another meeting to clarify details or getting started date.

I want to focus on steps 2 & 3 of my 12 steps. They are crucial to setting the scene for the meeting – particularly if it is the first time you have done it. Here's what you say to put their mind at ease and frame the meeting.

> *"You're probably wondering why I am here. First of all there is nothing to worry about and as (admin person's name) would have told you there is no charge for this meeting. The reason I am here is that I feel, as a firm, we have been neglecting you. All we have really offered you in the past has been basic compliance services. We've always wanted to offer more and the reality is, due to excessive compliance work, we have never really been a position to offer our other services that really make a difference to your profit, cashflow and overall wealth.*
>
> *To rectify our errors and to make amends, for the past few months we have been creating capacity so we can get out and see clients, understand their business more and, if appropriate, really help them achieve greater results in business and in life.*
>
> *So this meeting is an exploratory meeting to really understand your situation / business and really understand what you want to do in the future.*
>
> *Did (name) say it would take this (X amount of time) – are you still OK with that?"*

And then you go into the meeting understanding their situation more and importantly the clients' objectives.

Don't be in too much of a hurry to tell them all the answers. You're going to sell them the answers in a written implementation plan. Make sure you have meetings 'back to back' and you stick to the allotted time which is typically around 90 minutes.

> Quotable quote:
>
> *"Make sure you have meetings 'back to back' and you stick to the allotted time which is typically around 90 minutes."*

Client meetings need to happen at least every 6 months. If you are a typical Partner of an Accounting firm then you'll have around 120 business clients. That averages out at 20 per Partner per month on average.

Proactive phone calls

Over a 2 year period I interviewed 1,077 business clients on behalf of 126 Accounting firms. There were approximately 8 clients per meeting in a 'client advisory board' format. The questions to the clients were primarily around what they like, don't like and what they would like to see improved or added if they were running the firm. The Partners were not in the room and I would give a report after the meeting. One of these meetings stood out. I got to the 'improvement of service' question when a paint retailer called Barry said the following:

> *"I would love it if the partner who looks after me, Greg, would phone me up from time to time and ask one simple question – how's business? I would tell him what is going on and who knows there could be an opportunity for Greg to help me and win some more business from me."*

This happened in a recorded meeting from a client! They want you to call them, send emails, letters or useful information pieces. How often are you proactively calling them with no agenda? I think for the clients you want to keep, you should call 3 - 4 times per year. You don't even have to speak with them. You could leave a message and say you're just checking in.

> Quotable quote:
>
> *"I would love it if the partner who looks after me, Greg, would phone me up from time to time and ask one simple question – how's business?"*

Ever since that client advisory board meeting I have been promoting proactive phone calls with a 'how is it going' agenda. The Accountants that do it are creating better relationships with their clients.

Not charging for communication

I still find it bizarre that Accountants want to charge for phone calls and meetings. I know of firms that have wanted to charge clients for receiving newsletters and travel time. I don't think there are too many (unlike your Legal colleagues) who still charge for letter writing, courier fees, faxing and other meaningless 'disbursements.'

Think about it. You want to build a better relationship with clients and building a relationship with a client takes communication. And you want to charge for communicating with them. What the…?

Imagine if you are a client who knows you charge for phone calls and meetings. Guess what? They will only call you when they absolutely have to. And they will want to keep the conversation short and not get involved in 'small talk' with the fear of being charged for the chit chat. What a wasted opportunity to find out what the client really needs. What a wasted opportunity to find out the client's deep problems and hidden opportunities.

The successful firms who are smashing it with growth are not charging for phone calls, emails and quick meetings. In fact they are telling the clients that they do not. They are using this as a differentiator against other firms.

Imagine if you get a call from a prospective client where they ask *'what are your charge rates and how do you charge?'* There are 2 ways you could answer that question:

Option 1:

'We charge by the hour for everything we do and the price per hour is dependent on who does your work. If you use the graduate they are $120 per hour. The senior is $160 per hour. The client manager is $220 per hour and as the Partner I charge $350 per hour.'

Option 2:

'Thanks for asking. Here at XYZ we don't have charge rates and as such we don't charge by the hour. The vast majority of accounting firms charge a graduating fee based on the skill levels of the people they use. They also typically charge for every phone call, email and meeting as well. We don't charge you for any of that. We charge you a set fee on each project that we agree on together before the project

starts. Included in every project are unlimited phone calls, emails and meetings for anyone who is working on the project. That way there are no surprises with the fee and no barriers to doing business with us. We want you to call or email us as many times as you need throughout our time together. We think that is a fairer way to do business for you.'

As a client of an accounting firm give me Option 2 any day. I have certainty of price and there are no barriers to picking up the phone or shooting off an email. Most Partners of Accounting firms think that clients will abuse the privilege. Let me assure you they will not. Even if you do not currently charge for phone calls, emails and meetings you must tell the clients. They think you are like every other Accounting firm.

> Quotable quote:
>
> *"Even if you do not currently charge for phone calls, emails and meetings you must tell the clients."*

The same goes for low value seminars, client advisory board invitations and social media. I know of some firms who want to (and sometimes do) charge their clients to attend their annual Christmas party. If the seminar has value then by all means charge. If it is a sales pitch then don't charge. Client Advisory Boards are an awesome way to communicate with clients. Social media is a tool to communicate with clients.

Stop thinking like a labor hire business where you have to charge for every interaction and minute on the clock. It'll keep you in the poor house.

For you to Remain Relevant and thrive you'll need to dramatically increase the communication levels with all of your clients. Communicate a lot first. Increase the fee levels later!

> Quotable quote:
>
> *"Stop thinking like a labor hire business where you have to charge for every interaction and minute on the clock."*

Retaining clients

Most firms have a high retention rate per client. That means their clients stay clients of the firm for a long period of time. Somehow the Accounting profession has got most of their clients bluffed that it is hard to change Accountants. It's actually not.

Partners will argue that clients remain with the firm because of the great relationship they have with their clients. I beg to differ. How can you have a great relationship with someone when you see them once or twice per year?

Imagine what your relationship would be like at home if you only saw your life partner once or twice per year? For some of you reading this it would be better!

I do not think retention rate is high because of great service, relationships, value for money or services offered. I think retention rate is high because of **financial intimacy.**

I think retention rate is high because you know things about the client's financial affairs that no one else does.

> Quotable quote:
>
> *"I do not think retention rate is high because of great service, relationships, value for money or services offered. I think retention rate is high because of **financial intimacy**."*

It's financial intimacy. Period. Most people do not speak openly about their financial affairs – it's a very private matter. And if they only speak to a couple of people about a very private matter a lot of trust is built up. Not relationship – trust.

Your clients trust you to not tell others. So they don't leave.

However, the real measure is how happy they are to be a client of your firm. I think that metric is based on the number of referrals you receive each year per client and how many projects they buy from you each year.

For starters, work out the average referrals per client. If you divided the number of referrals (enquiries) you get annually into your total client base this will give you a startling reality of how happy your clients actually are.

Now the flip side to that is they may want you all for themselves and they do not want to refer! Possibly. The easiest way to increase the number of referrals is to systematically ask for them. If you deserve a referral (great service, etc.) then you'll get referrals. Most clients do not refer for 3 reasons:

> Quotable quote:
>
> *"The easiest way to increase the number of referrals is to systematically ask for them."*

1. You've never asked – we didn't know you wanted any
2. You seem to be too busy – we don't want our service levels to drop
3. We're not happy – something has happened in the past

If you focus on those 3 then you'll get more referrals. This chapter is not about marketing and referrals it's about clients and WOWing them into staying with you.

Focusing on retaining clients is not about increasing the retention rate, it's about making memorable experiences with existing clients so they buy more from you and refer more to you.

As a measure of great retention you should be aiming for an actual retention rate of 95%, at least 1 referral per client per year and at least 4 projects per client purchased each year.

Let's explore the **number of projects per year** that clients buy from you.

The more projects a client buys from you the better they are served and the more you 'put a fence' around the client. It makes it harder for them to leave your firm if they are buying (on average) 4+ services from you.

This KPI however should not be about retaining clients (although that will happen); it should be about

> Quotable quote:
>
> *"The more projects a client buys from you the better they are served and the more you 'put a fence' around the client."*

servicing them properly. The internal mantra should be *'all clients are buying every service they need that helps them achieve their goals.'*

If you are doing your job currently by building close relationships with your clients, meeting them frequently at no cost, you will get to know them and you will find many projects and opportunities.

To work out the number of projects per client take your invoices sent number and divide the number of clients into it. Typically it will be around 2 projects per client per year.

Here's a simple test. In a table, list all your services across the top and all your clients on the left hand side. Apply a 'tick' or a 'cross' to each client and each product and see how many ticks you come up with. This is a measure of your 'product penetration.' It's called a client product matrix. It looks like this:

CLIENT / PRODUCT MATRIX

	Corp Secretarial	Annual Accounts	FBT / Other Tax	SMSF / 401k Audit	Budget	CashFlow	Planning Session	Monitoring - mthly / quarterly	Tax Planning	Health Check	Asset Protection	Coaching	Systems Development
Client Name	✓	✓	✓	✗	✗	✗	✗	✗	✗	✗	✗	✗	✗
Client Name	✓	✓	✗	✗	✓	✓	✗	✓	✗	✗	✗	✗	✗
Client Name	✓	✓	✓	✓	✗	✗	✗	✗	✗	✗	✗	✗	✓
Client Name	✓	✓	✗	✗	✗	✗	✗	✓	✗	✓	✗	✗	✗
Client Name	✓	✓	✓	✗	✗	✗	✗	✗	✓	✗	✗	✗	✗
Client Name	✓	✓	✗	✓	✗	✗	✗	✗	✗	✗	✗	✓	✗
Client Name	✓	✓	✗	✗	✗	✗	✗	✓	✗	✗	✗	✗	✗
Client Name	✓	✓	✓	✓	✗	✗	✗	✗	✗	✗	✗	✓	✗

My guess is that less than 15% of your clients buy every service you have to offer! Yet many clients need your additional services – they just don't know they exist because you have never offered them. What an opportunity!

If you have a focus on 'all clients you want to keep' then you will make sure they are buying what they need to succeed. A systematic approach is needed with a consistent questioning and interview process.

> Quotable quote:
>
> *"Another measure of your retention rate is how much the **average project value** is per client. The higher it is the happier they are."*

Another measure of your retention rate is how much the **average project value** is per client. The higher it is the happier they are.

A project is not the annual fee with a client. Annual accounting is a project. A business plan is a project. A finance proposal is a project. A tax return is a project.

What is your average project value? It's simple to work out. All you need to do is divide the number of invoices sent into your revenue for the year. If you have multiple invoices for one project then that should be classed as one invoice.

Your average project value multiplied by the number of projects per client per year will equal your revenue per client.

It's a great way to look at your client base. If you have a very small average project value (but lots of clients) you will have a large administration function just for invoicing. With a small average project value you will also have a higher than normal attrition rate – it's no big deal if they leave.

The objective should be to increase the average project value whilst increasing the number of projects that each client buys from you each year. If your business clients are not spending at least $10,000 with you annually and buying at least 4 projects from you (therefore the average project value is around $2,500) then I think you are massively under-servicing your client base.

As you work out your numbers for your firm it might look something like this:

Revenue	$2,000,000
Invoices sent	639
Average project value	$3,129.89
Number of clients	192
Number of projects per client	3.3
Average fee per client	$10,416.67

You have low attrition because of high financial intimacy. You get higher financial intimacy by delivering amazing service and making sure every client is buying every product they need that helps them achieve their goals.

Keeping a watchful eye on clients every day

Disclaimer: The product you are about to read about is owned by my company.

I love the way cloud technology is shaping the future of the Accounting profession. I love it because for the first time in history you can 'see' what is happening in your client base as it is happening. If the client is on a cloud Accounting system as they are transacting every day, their software is automatically being updated with those transactions.

As they make a sale, buy inventory, pay an invoice and receive money from a customer it is all getting updated. Since you are the trusted advisor you have access to their accounting system. That means you can go and look into their finances every day if you choose. If you wanted to look you could spot trends, issues and opportunities. With your analytic Accounting hat on you could even predict major issues before it happened. It is very hard to do that if your client is on an old-fashioned 'hard drive' based accounting system.

> Quotable quote:
>
> *"One of the challenges you'll have when a lot of your clients migrate their old systems across to the new cloud system is the volume of data that you can now potentially see."*

This is a very good reason to promote cloud accounting to your clients. One of the challenges you'll have when a lot of your clients migrate their old systems across to the new cloud system is the volume of data that you can now potentially see.

You can overcome this by consolidating all of your clients cloud data (from multiple accounting packages) into one easy to read dashboard. You can do that with tools like PANALITIX (www.panalitix.com) and it will even alert you when your client KPI's drop below or rise above certain preset levels.

When you see what is going on (good and bad) you could send

them a quick email or text or call them in for a meeting if something 'untoward' is happening. You might have noticed that sales have dropped, inventory has risen, receivables have increased and cash has gone down. It looks like they are in for a cashflow grind if they are not already in one.

This sort of intelligence is very cool and it will help you deliver the ultimate in client service.

For over 20 years I have been advocating that you need to be proactive. It's actually quite hard and frustrating to get Accountants to do that. With cool tools like PANALITIX that alert you to what is going on you no longer need to be proactive. All you need to do is react (tongue firmly in cheek) to what you see in front of you. Just do it every day!

Delivering WOW every day

I have been telling Accountants to be Proactive and Add Value ever since I started working with you in May 1994.

If you are going to Remain Relevant you are going to have to be **proactive and add value**. That means the level of WOW needs to improve.

They leave you for another firm because of the following reasons:

1. **Service** – the client service experience was poor
2. **Services** – the value for money was poor or they thought they needed more but not getting it

The services must be complete (all clients buying every service they need that helps them achieve their goals) and the customer service must be WOW.

Here's the thing. If an Accountant 'sees' an issue or opportunity in the client details then they are obliged to tell the client. The problem is most Accountants are 'store blind' and are not focused on seeing ways to really help clients.

> Quotable quote:
>
> "If an Accountant 'sees' an issue or opportunity in the client details then they are obliged to tell the client."

Here are some quick thoughts on how you can add value to what you are doing:

1. Offer free phone calls/emails and meetings all year
2. Conduct a Business Performance Review every year with every client
3. Conduct a 'finding opportunities' brainstorming exercise on every client every year
4. Create a closed networking group on one of the social media platforms and connect your clients
5. Visit every client 2 times per year (free) to see how you can help
6. Call every client 4 times per year (free) to touch base and see how they are going
7. Run client advisory boards to get feedback from clients on how you can improve
8. Run seminars and workshops and teach the clients something new

I came up with that list in 5 minutes! Ask your team what else you can do and create your 'adding value list.' Your team might focus on customer service ideas like:

> Quotable quote:
>
> *"Call every client 4 times per year (free) to touch base and see how they are going"*

- ✓ Offering beverages and food with a menu upon arrival
- ✓ Following up on every interaction with a quick call
- ✓ Writing a thank you note when they pay their bill on time
- ✓ Remembering their name when they come in
- ✓ Putting their name on the 'welcome board' for every visit
- ✓ Having a 'lollie/candy salad' on the front counter
- ✓ Calling them on their birthday
- ✓ Sending cards/gifts at appropriate times throughout the year
- ✓ Having fresh flowers in the office
- ✓ Sending snippets from newspapers/magazines that may interest them
- ✓ Letting your clients know when you'll be finishing their project and exceeding the deadline
- ✓ Return phone call and other communication the same day.

I am sure your team can come up with many more. The service levels in the profession are fairly poor so it's not hard to deliver WOW service every day.

Chapter 6
Productizing what you know

The IP purveying business

Every time I do a seminar and ask the question 'what do you sell?' the answer is always the same. They either say knowledge, solutions, me or ideas. I completely agree this is what you sell. However the vast majority of business models of Accounting firms suggest they sell 'time.' Keeping an accurate check on time and making sure every minute is recorded and hopefully on-charged to clients. The business model suggests that you own a 'labor hire' business rather than and intellectual property purveying business.

If you persist with the labor hire business model then you need more people, bigger offices and more hassles. **All of that stinks of effort!**

A far better way is to package what you know in different ways and sell what you know over and over again – with the least amount of labor possibly. As a customer of an Accounting firm I am not buying time from you – I am buying what you know.

> Quotable quote:
>
> *"As a customer of an Accounting firm I am not buying time from you – I am buying what you know."*

You and I are no different. I know things that you don't know and you know things that I don't know. I just choose to package and sell what I know in different and highly leveraged ways. I have been in the intellectual property purveying business since 1993. I have always taken what I know and packaged it so it could be delivered in a leveraged way. There is only one me so I have to. Since 1993 I worked as an employee for 6 years and the rest of the time I have owned my own businesses. Since 1993 I have been directly involved in creating, marketing, selling and delivering over $170M of productized and packaged knowledge. I wish it was all profit!

Here is a list of the types of products I have created and/or delivered over the years (I am not including the free giveaways just the ones that were sold):

- ✓ Seminars & small workshops
- ✓ Multi day workshops
- ✓ Multi day conferences
- ✓ Client advisory board meetings
- ✓ Team advisory board meetings
- ✓ Round table briefing session
- ✓ Keynote speeches
- ✓ Audio tapes in a box
- ✓ VHS video in a box
- ✓ CD audio recording in a box
- ✓ DVD training programs in a box
- ✓ Books, manuals & reports – hard copy and e-copy
- ✓ Group based coaching & mentoring
- ✓ Group based consulting
- ✓ Franchise system
- ✓ Phone / web based Business Performance Review
- ✓ In office training sessions
- ✓ E-learning platform
- ✓ Posters and wall charts
- ✓ 90-day business challenge
- ✓ Webinar series
- ✓ Conference call series
- ✓ Software

Every one of these products were delivered with leverage in mind. Some required a little labor and many required no labor at all to deliver them. Labor based delivery products stink of effort.

Every single one of these products could have been delivered 'one on one' but I chose not to do that. I am in the IP purveying business just like you. I am not in the 'time selling' business. The time selling business stinks of effort.

Did all of them work? Not at all. Some are still active today and many are not. I take what we (my business partner Colin and our team) know and we look to use it over and over again in different delivery mediums. If it works we keep

> Quotable quote:
>
> *"If it doesn't work we pull the product and do something else."*

doing it in that format. If it doesn't work we pull the product and do something else.

To come up with ideas for products we look at 3 areas.

1. The situation (why create a product in the first place)
2. What we know (our knowledge base)
3. The innovation (the actual product)

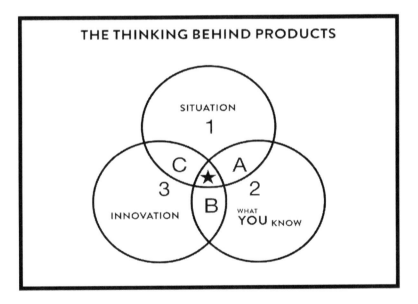

When all 3 are in sync the product works. Points 2 and 3 will be dealt with later in this chapter. For now I want to talk about the situation. The situation (that forces you to create a product in the first place) could be negative based or opportunistic based.

You could have a negative situation that was out of your control and you want to recover from that. You could have an opportunistic situation that you see and you want to capitalize on.

NEGATIVE	OPPORTUNISTIC
Rising salary costs	Government legislation change
Cashflow problems (yours)	Technology (cloud) movement
Lost clients	New tax changes
Recessionary or hard times	Niche markets you want to target
Clients cashflow problems	Trends in an industry
Revenue declining	Offshore labor availability
Team members leaving	Selling your business
Increased expenses	Client demands / needs
Competition	Capitalism

The situation is what forces you to act. There needs to be a trigger of some sort as to why you want to make changes. Sometimes the situation is survival based and sometimes it is purely an idea that you think the market might need.

The Accounting profession is being threatened by many outside forces. For the profession to Remain Relevant it needs to realize that it is in the intellectual property creating, marketing, selling and delivery business. With labor rates increasing every year and new nimble players appearing daily (who do realize this) it is a non-negotiable.

> Quotable quote:
> "For the profession to Remain Relevant it needs to realize that it is in the intellectual property creating, marketing, selling and delivery business."

Just realizing it is not enough, the business model needs to change to capitalize on the future.

Sell what you know

What you currently know is the starting point. What knowledge do you have and what knowledge does your team have?

This is an interesting exercise. To create this segment I spent 20 minutes coming up with a list of what my team and I know. It is not a definitive list but it is a decent one.

How to improve/develop/implement/create...

- ✓ Cashflow
- ✓ Profit
- ✓ Team
- ✓ Lower attrition
- ✓ Higher morale
- ✓ Improved image
- ✓ Turnaround time
- ✓ Strategy
- ✓ Marketing
- ✓ Sales
- ✓ Value added services
- ✓ Accountants receivable
- ✓ Pricing
- ✓ Work in progress
- ✓ Seminars
- ✓ Webinars
- ✓ Product Development
- ✓ Software creation
- ✓ Copywriting
- ✓ Team structure
- ✓ Coaching – phone & group
- ✓ Consulting
- ✓ Training
- ✓ Presenting
- ✓ Conferences
- ✓ Social media
- ✓ Branding

- ✓ Digital media
- ✓ DVD products
- ✓ Outsourcing
- ✓ Cloud Technology
- ✓ Sales management
- ✓ CRM
- ✓ Benchmarking
- ✓ Group planning
- ✓ Content management
- ✓ Database creation
- ✓ Telemarketing
- ✓ Higher productivity
- ✓ Better performance
- ✓ Market share
- ✓ Revenue growth
- ✓ Wealth improvement
- ✓ Innovation
- ✓ Efficiency
- ✓ Problem solving
- ✓ Customer service
- ✓ Online business model
- ✓ How to implement
- ✓ +++

What do you currently know? Get your team involved (I did not get my team involved to create this list) and see if you can come up with a definitive list.

To create a leveraged productized business it all starts with what you know.

What products can be created

If you are following what I am saying here we are moving away from the 'time selling' business and into the productized IP business. The first step is to work out what you know and the second step is work out what the package looks like.

Most Accountants I meet believe that there are opportunities for additional business in their current client base. However, they don't seem that active in discovering the opportunities nor promoting the services. I think it is a BIG dis-service to the client if you do not promote new ideas and new services.

We recommend that you *stay close to the numbers* with your service offerings. That way you can leverage the delivery of the services to other team members. By all means offer high level consulting, however typically that means that very experienced (read expensive) people need to deliver them.

One of the reasons Accountants do not offer additional services is because they are unsure what the client will say and they doubt if they have the knowledge base to deliver the solution.

You have to differentiate between coaching and consulting. Consulting is where the provider comes up with the answers, coaching is where the client is guided and the answers are coached out of the client.

Financial coaching is the way to go. We recommend that your service categories fall in 8 areas. We call it the Awesome 8! It's what your clients are interested in – over and above compliance services.

> Quotable quote:
>
> *"Consulting is where the provider comes up with the answers, coaching is where the client is guided and the answers are coached out of the client."*

THE AWESOME 8

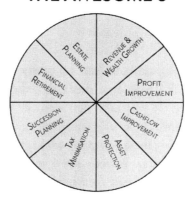

If you follow the Awesome 8 then here are 20 new services you could create:

1. Revenue growth program
2. Cash flow analysis, forecasting & monitoring program
3. Profit improvement program
4. Debt re-structuring program
5. Receivables management service
6. Inventory management service
7. Bookkeeping (serviced from lower cost countries)
8. Virtual Management Accounting
9. Cloud conversions
10. Sort out the numbers program
11. Monitoring & Accountability program
12. Webinar / Seminar / Workshops / events
13. Planning sessions – face2face, group or remote
14. Boxed product (DVD, etc.) for a niche market
15. Books / Manuals / Podcasts / Video subscriptions
16. Software or online learning – subscription based
17. Challenges – 100 day / 6 week, etc.
18. Leveraged training or consulting
19. Group coaching
20. Cashflow in a Crisis program

At the end of the day **every client should be buying every product they need that helps them achieve their goals!**
That should be your goal.

Build the plane as you fly it

I have noticed that Accountants can be pretty good procrastinators. Really you say! I think it's because they <u>think</u> they need to get it right before getting started. If you take that attitude then you'll never get anything off the ground.

There was once a dog food company who invented the 'world's best dog food'. It had everything perfect – the texture, the smell, the protein and fat content, etc. It even had amazing packaging and the dog food company was able to get onto the supermarket shelves at eye level. After a massive marketing campaign the dog owners bought the product with hope and enthusiasm. They fed the product to their beloved dogs however **the dogs didn't like it.** The company went broke because they let perfect get in the way of success.

What I like to do is 'write the brochure first' before I create any new product. What I mean by that is I will draft the promise, the website or the sales letter and then do some marketing to see if my market wants to buy it. Then I'll create the product. I don't want to waste my resources creating something if no one is going to buy it. I like to build the plane as we fly it.

> Quotable quote:
>
> *"What I like to do is 'write the brochure first' before I create any new product."*

Creating products and productizing your Accounting firm need not be difficult. There are 8 questions to ask and implement:

1. What do you know?
2. Who is it applicable to?
3. How will it be packaged?
4. What technology is needed?
5. How will it be marketed?
6. How will it be sold?
7. How will be implemented?
8. How will it be supported?

On a nimble, low-cost model we implement new product ideas all the time. They don't always work. Sometimes the dogs don't like it. A great example of that was the '**Rob doll' action figure** – not a big seller!

You have to be prepared to cut your losses fast when you start creating and promoting products. Not everything will work as planned. Just because you like it doesn't mean your market will. You can't pre-judge who will buy and

> Quotable quote:
>
> *"You can't pre-judge who will buy and who will not. With your best marketing give everyone the chance to buy what you have."*

who will not. With your best marketing give everyone the chance to buy what you have.

If you're onto something that is working then get testimonials / case studies from happy clients (we call them WHAM's – written happy Accountants moments) and leverage those so you can sell more. Keep testing different methods of explaining, promoting, packaging and pricing until you get it close to being right. Then rinse and repeat. Over and over and over again!

Chapter 7
Let's make some targeted noise

Your marketing objectives

What's the point of having a great service offering, fantastic client results, great people and an inspiring vision if only you and your team know about it? Your business might be a finely tuned instrument but if it is not played in the orchestra then no-one will hear it.

It's time to make some noise, make some music and tell the world (including your existing clients) how good you are and what you can do for them. It's time to do some marketing!

Before I get into my definition of marketing I need to clear up a misconception in the market place as to what marketing is and what the purpose is. Many people think marketing is all about 'getting the word out there' or 'building awareness' or 'branding.' Yes, they are all important and they need to be done. However unless you understand the core purpose of marketing and what it is all about you will waste a lot of time and a lot of money on activities that do not work.

My definition of marketing is **'Marketing is salesmanship multiplied.'** The purpose of marketing is to sell your message in a leveraged way so that people respond to it. The purpose of marketing is invoke a response. Hopefully a positive one.

If you think a billboard / ad / flyer with your firm's name, a catchy phrase

> Quotable quote:
>
> *"The purpose of marketing is to sell your message in a leveraged way so that people respond to it."*

and a picture of your Partners sells what your firm can do for me then good luck to you. It's not going to work. The only people who get excited by that are the Partners – provided the photo is good. It'll be a waste of time and a BIG waste of money. But the Partners will feel good.

If you think a 6 page full color brochure of your people, the brand values, your premises, your services offered and how many years you have been in business is going to work then think again. Again, you'll feel good about the glossy brochure but it won't work.

> **Quotable quote:**
>
> *"If you think a 6 page full color brochure of your people, the brand values, your premises, your services offered and how many years you have been in business is going to work then think again."*

Everything you do in your marketing efforts must be about sales in a leveraged way. By leverage I mean the medium you use (email, video, paper, seminar, etc.) and the volume of people who see it.

The message you need to be selling is social proof and the results I get when I use you. In other words by responding to your promotion how I will be better off. It's all about the radio station that has been around since the dawn of the slate tablet – W.I.I.F.M. What's in it for me?

Q. Why should I enquire?
Q. Why should I respond?
Q. Why should I download?
Q. Why should I attend?

I don't care that you have been in business since 1973 and you are all Chartered Accountants. What I care about it is where's the value to me!

With my definition as 'salesmanship multiplied' it is not a marketing functions job to make a sale. Very few people buy professional services from a marketing message. They buy professional services from a person.

The job of the marketing message is to sell the idea that I should respond to find out more. ...Hmmm, that sounds good; I'll make an enquiry/click the button/attend the seminar/pick up the phone and make contact....

Marketing is about selling a dream, hope and future possibilities. As

I said marketing is about invoking a response. In other words marketing needs to be in the style of 'direct response.' You send out a marketing message and you get a response. Branding is important and it must be done but it shouldn't be the primary focus.

Direct response marketing has been around a long time and any seasoned marketer will tell you that it is not an instant gratification process. It takes time. It doesn't work the first time. I hear so many Partners of firms say *'we sent out 1 invite to my seminar and it didn't work.'* And then they give up. Paaalllllleeeeese!

Marketing needs to be a consistent approach that assists in the growing of revenue and profits. There is no point doing marketing when you are quiet. It takes a while to 'crank it up.' You need to be marketing all of the time. That means every day!

> Quotable quote:
>
> *"Marketing needs to be a consistent approach that assists in the growing of revenue and profits."*

Many firms start their marketing journey with no real objectives in mind. Now I know 'build brand awareness' and 'get our name out there' are objectives but they are hard to measure (and ALL marketing must be measured) the real objective is to 'get their name in here' while you build your brand.

> Quotable quote:
>
> *"To grow your numbers you'll certainly need the right skills, the right tools and the right people in place."*

Your marketing assists your sales function. It comes before sales. Marketing generates an enquiry and then the sales function closes the enquiry into new business. A finely tuned marketing and sales machine can grow all sorts of numbers. To grow your numbers you'll certainly need the right skills, the right tools and the right people in place.

At the outset you need to set your objectives. Which numbers do you want to grow? Take the chart below as an example. Your marketing and sales function combined can directly influence all 15 of these numbers. If you work out what your base is (and it is what it is) then set some targets and then get active.

MARKETING & SALES OBJECTIVES	NOW	12 MONTHS
1. Number of client groups		
2. Number of projects each client buys from you each year		
3. Average project value - $		
4. Average fee per client (2 x 3) - $		
5. Percentage of total revenue in compliance - %		
6. Percentage of total revenue in advisory - %		
7. Average hourly rate / Realization margin in compliance - $		
8. Average hourly rate / Realization margin in advisory - $		
9. Number of new enquiries generated per year		
10. Conversion rate of enquiry to sale		
11. Number of new clients per year		
12. Each client visited / met with – times per year		
13. Number of clients on cloud accounting system		
14. Revenue - $		
15. Profit / EBIT before partner salaries - $		

I get asked all the time *'how much marketing should I do?'* or, *'when should I hire a marketing person?'*.

My answer is always the same. It depends what your objectives are. You may think that even with a small growth target of 5% that you do not need to do any marketing. Think again. You cannot rely on some reactive referrals and a charge rate increase to grow anymore. What I outlined in my Dear Accountant letter and chapter 1 is that you'll need to do some marketing just to maintain your current revenue.

If you wanted to double your current revenue then the chart below shows what your annual growth rate needs to be.

$1,000,000	ANNUAL GROWTH RATE BEFORE YOUR REVENUE DOUBLES					
YEARS	**7.5%**	**10%**	**12.5%**	**15%**	**20%**	**26%**
1	$1,075,000	$1,100,000	$1,125,000	$1,150,000	$1,200,000	$1,260,000
2	$1,155,625	$1,210,000	$1,265,625	$1,322,500	$1,440,000	$1,587,600
3	$1,242,297	$1,331,000	$1,435,629	$1,520,875	$1,728,000	$2,000,376
4	$1,335,469	$1,464,100	$1,601,807	$1,749,006	$2,073,600	
5	$1,435,629	$1,610,510	$1,802,032	$2,011,357		
6	$1,543,302	$1,771,561	$2,027,287			
7	$1,659,049	$1,948,717				
8	$1,783,478	$2,143,589				
9	$1,917,239					
10	$2,061,032					

Growth is a good thing. It shows health, vitality and innovation. You decide how fast you want to grow over what period of time. Whatever your growth targets are (even if it's a plodding 5% goal) you'll more than likely need to do some marketing.

Think of marketing like a wheel barrow. It only works if you push it. The more marketing you do the more choices you have.

Niche markets – your best buyer

Someone once said ... '*If you are everything to everyone then you are nothing to nobody.*' I don't know who said but it sums up my thoughts on who you should target as clients. I am a big fan of having clients in niche markets. I am a big fan of knowing who your 'best buyer' is, what they look like and where they hang out.

To help you determine your best buyer the key questions to ask are: *If there was a room full of my best buyers in front of me....*

a. What would they look like?
b. Where would they come from?
c. What do they do?
d. What are they interested in?
e. What services do they need to buy?
f. What size (revenue / wealth) are they?
g. How old are they?
h. What is their risk profile?
i. What is their ambition level?

You are describing your ideal client. Your best buyer. Once you understand the demographics of your target market you can target better, you can become an expert in their industry and you can command higher fees. Ultimately you are more useful to your clients if you know more about them. Your services can be tailored to your niche. Your marketing can be tailored to your niche.

> Quotable quote:
>
> "*Once you understand the demographics of your target market you can target better, you can become an expert in their industry and you can command higher fees.*"

Your niche could be based on geography, service offering, behavior, industry type or a mix.

- **Geographic niche** – we are the small business experts in New Zealand
- **Services niche** – we help business owners to be financially retired
- **Behavior niche** – we help Entrepreneurs start and then exit their businesses
- **Industry niche** – we help Restaurateurs to grow and develop their businesses
- **Mixed niche** – we help Entrepreneurial Restaurant owners in New Zealand to start their businesses, develop their businesses and get them to a point where the owner is financially retired from their business.

My niche market is very clear to me and my team.

We help Accounting firms of all sizes around the world who are active in cloud accounting grow and develop their firms as well as help them to offer valuable business advisory services to their clients.

So for me it helps us get very focused. We are global. We are servicing Accounting firms (not Accountants in commerce) of all sizes. We are on the lookout for firms active in cloud accounting. We are interested in firms who want to grow and develop their firms. And we are most interested in firms who want to take business advisory services to their clients.

If that sounds like you then please be in touch. We'd love to show you what we do. The articulation of our niche helps us make decisions on product development, marketing, sales and support.

I have 4 rules when selecting a niche market to target:

1. **Are there lots of them?** You may like the '*Mangalitsa Pig*' because they are wooly and a rare breed of pig. I am sure there are farmers who specialize in the growing and developing of said pig. However, I highly doubt there are that many farmers. I think your niche market needs at least 5,000 of them in your chosen geographical region.

2. **Do they have the ability to pay?** There may be thousands of 'lawn mowing' people (with the greatest respect to the people that mow our lawns) however by and large they don't earn much money and they may not have the ability to pay your fees. You need to select a niche that either has money now or has the ability to make money. You are not a charity!

3. **Can you make a difference to them?** The services you offer your niche need to be valuable services and the success of them (clients improved condition) needs to be measured. You need to make a difference so they keep paying you and you can get case studies from them. It also helps with your personal enjoyment.

> Quotable quote:
>
> *"You need to make a difference so they keep paying you and you can get case studies from them."*

4. **Are they enjoyable to work with?** You are going to spend a considerable amount of your waking professional life with these people. You need to at least like their company. Within any demographic there are always miserable people who are negative whiners who complain about everything. Just cut them out of your list once you find them!

Work out who your best buyer is, what they look like, where they hang out and go and get them.

You…an object of interest

We don't buy professional services from 'faceless' companies that have no personality. People buy from people they know, like and trust.

I am about to choose an Accounting firm to entrust my financial affairs with. We are about to get 'intimate' on my finances and I want to make sure that you are who you say you are and you are worthy of trusting.

The reason clients stay with Accounting firms is not because of the service or the services (however we will leave if they are bad) it's because of the financial intimacy that you have with me. You know things about my financial affairs that very few people do. We are loyal to our Accountants and we want them to be similar to us. Well, sort of like us.

> Quotable quote:
>
> *"We are loyal to our Accountants and we want them to be similar to us."*

If I am a boring person who likes beige (not to offend anyone who is a beige fan) then I will **not** choose a flamboyant Accountant who wears floral, gold bling and drives a Lamborghini. I would like to choose someone who is a bit more conservative. Maybe that is your target market. Not right, not wrong.

If I am an Entrepreneur who likes to be creative, invent new things, is tech savvy then I will most certainly **not** pick an Accountant who does wear beige, a woolen cardigan and slip on soft sole shoes. I am looking for a bit more pizazz and flair, some funky offices and cool people in the office.

What if I am a professional and I run a professional services firm. Most are not overly Entrepreneurial and they will be very interested in your 'heritage.' Which schools you went to, what qualifications you have and which clubs you are part of and so on. They are **not** about to pick the racy, Entrepreneurial type Accountant (with sometimes dubious qualifications) who likes to push the envelope.

What if I am a blue collar worker – a tradesperson. I am a hard worker who likes to get dirty and who works hard. I may not have a university degree so I don't want to be intimidated by those that have 3 of them.

Your clients are a reflection of you. They are typically 10 years in age either side of you and they act in similar ways to you. If you know that then you can do something about targeting them. You can design your office, your car, your dress sense, your mannerisms, your travel schedule, your service offerings, your team and your marketing.

> Quotable quote:
>
> *"Your clients are a reflection of you. They are typically 10 years in age either side of you and they act in similar ways to you."*

You can become an object of interest to your current and future clients.

Accountants are supposed to be the leaders of business. At least that's what the profession would like to think. I think Accountants can be leaders of business but if they are, they need to walk the walk. People like to look up to leaders. They like to put them on a pedestal and admire them.

There's an old truth in leadership…

> *"In a pack of dogs if you're not the lead dog*
> *then the view is always the same"*

As a leader you have an obligation to practice what you preach. So do not talk to me about wealth creation if you do not have the signs of wealth. Do not talk to me about business improvement if yours clearly needs improving.

> Quotable quote:
> "In a pack of dogs if you're not the lead dog then the view is always the same"

If people like to follow interesting people then why don't you become one? Why doesn't your firm become interesting?

It's a 'sea of sameness' out there and it doesn't take much to stand out from the crowd.

In many countries the 'tall poppy syndrome' exists. That means that in a field of poppies the tall ones get chopped down first. It is real and some people will attempt to 'bring you down to size' but hey – are they your target clients? Probably not.

I believe I am an object of interest to a lot of people. I have designed it that way. In doing so *I get hate mail.* It's quite frequent and it's been happening over a long period of time. I write and comment on matters in the Accounting profession that upset some people. I tend to tell it the way it is and I am not scared of doing so. The 'hate mail' can be in the form of a letter, a fax, a feedback form, an email and sometimes on social media. Sometimes it's a phone call or verbal abuse face to face. I am very polite but they ultimately get the standard response of 'delete' and I never hear from them again. Bring on the hate mail I say. Everyone is entitled to their opinion. And by all means give me yours. I know I am right and the 'hate mailer' is wrong. I know what I stand for and I am not afraid to say it.

Being an object of interest gets you fans and it gets you detractors. Being an object of interest gets you a lot of business.

Web dominance

I am willing to bet that the vast majority of clients you currently have were referred to you by an existing client. A referral from a trusted source is a very powerful marketing tool. That method of 'lead source' will continue into the future. However, it's changing. There are still people involved and now so is the Internet.

> Quotable quote:
>
> *"A referral from a trusted source is a very powerful marketing tool."*

The Internet is a massive connection tool. It connects people, devices, opinions, thoughts, interests, hobbies and information. It can be a platform for building a brand and destroying a brand – sometimes in the same day. People (prospective team members, alliances or suppliers) can 'check you out' before doing business with you. The Internet is where we go to search, explore and generally get any information on anything we want. It's an awesome way to distribute content. It's an amazing way to promote your business. It is your 'shop window' to the world.

What does your Internet presence say about you and your firm?

If I search your name or your firm's name what do I find? Do I find you at all? When I do find you? Do I see a website that is old, tired and looks like it was a 'template' site? Or do I find a modern site that encourages me to stay for a while and get engaged? Do you only have one site or do you have multiple sites? Are you only on LinkedIn or can I find you on other social media platforms as well? Can I experience some of your content (or your most recent speech) on YouTube and can I see cases studies and testimonials of your clients somewhere?

The Internet is there to be leveraged and if you really want to grow your firm then you need to **dominate the web**. You need to dominate your space that you want to operate in.

> Quotable quote:
>
> *"The Internet is there to be leveraged and if you really want to grow your firm then you need to **dominate the web**."*

When I go on any popular platform and search for you, your business or your product / service then I find you. You're on the first page of Google and you seem to be 'everywhere.' I can view a video, download an opinion paper, use a calculator on your website, read an article or your most recent blog post.

I get Accountants who say 'do you think it is worthwhile having a presence on Facebook, Twitter and LinkedIn?' Please do not ask me that question again. Yes, Yes and Yes. It is not one platform, it is all platforms.

The table below shows a scoring system on each of the main areas you need to dominate. The first thing you need to do is mark in each box where you're at.

- Non-existent – pretty self-explanatory – you have nothing in this channel
- Existent – you have a presence in this channel
- Competitive – you are there and you are competitive against others in the same channel
- Distinct – you are there and you are different from others in the same channel
- Breakthrough – you are leading the charge and doing something different in this channel

WEB DOMINANCE					
WEB STRATEGY	**NON-EXISTENT**	**EXISTENT**	**COMPETITIVE**	**DISTINCT**	**BREAKTHROUGH**
Main website					
Feeder sites					
Blog(s)					
Facebook					
Twitter					
LinkedIn					
YouTube					
E-news					
Forum – connecting					
Search Engine Optimization					
Social advertising					
Other people's blogs					
Content marketing					

Let's look at each one:

Main website

The best main websites are those that have client case studies (video preferable), people (with photos) who can help me, content I can download / view, loads of testimonials, sign up pages to newsletters, outcomes of buying services from you and most important they are not boring. Make it fun, interactive and remember it is your shop window and a sales tool.

Feeder sites

Why limit yourself to just one website? Why not have other sites that are selling parts of what you do. You could have seminar sites, product sites, niche market sites, geographic sites, content specialty sites, etc. Think of what people may search for and create a website around that. They can all link together or feed into the main site. Each site is a mini sales tool in its own right.

Blog(s)

Writing a blog does not need to be a tiresome task. I started writing my blog (**www.robnixon.com**) in 2010 to put my thoughts on my platform. I average just over one new post per week. Sometimes I do 2-3 posts in a week, sometimes I skip a week. What's important is that I am blogging. I am writing about current ideas, methods, celebrations and the occasional promotion. If you want to be a thought leader you need to blog. If you want to dominate the web then you need something to say.

> Quotable quote:
> *"If you want to be a thought leader you need to blog. If you want to dominate the web then you need something to say."*

Facebook

It's free, easy and it's another platform you should be on. Many people think that Facebook is a 'personal only' platform. I disagree. It's a platform to bring out your personality. It's a platform to show that you 'are living large.' It's a platform to show travel and other interests. It's a platform to show off your family and your sporting prowess – or lack thereof it. Remember people buy from people – real people. Get a funky company page set up. Email all of your clients to 'like it' and actively seek out your clients to 'friend' with. But please, no pictures of your food. You can connect with me on Facebook - rob.nixon.969.

Twitter

It's a 140 character blogging site that works – if you work it. Many of your clients might be on Twitter but you'll never know unless you are. A daily 'tweet' can take less than 60 seconds. You can get a 'social media enhancer' person working from home to do it for you. One of the cool things about Twitter is you can link from your short tweet to other websites – yours! You can connect with me on Twitter - @therobnixon.

LinkedIn

The original intention of LinkedIn was to connect the world's Professionals. That is one of the reasons so many Accountants are on the platform. LinkedIn is a platform which has been disrupting the recruitment industry for a long time. It can also disrupt the Accounting profession. LinkedIn has a massive amount

> Quotable quote:
> "LinkedIn has a massive amount of content and you can post your content as well."

of content and you can post your content as well. It's a very sophisticated tool for finding people. It's a great tool for targeting companies you want as clients. Again, like all of these platforms you need to 'work it, baby' and post regularly and add value to the reader. You can connect with me on LinkedIn – therobnixon.

YouTube

I love YouTube (in a professional sense) because with a standard smartphone I can create a video quickly, upload to YouTube and then I can go to other platforms and tell the world about it. Making noise with video based marketing is super cool because I can get to know you a bit before I decide to enquire or buy. Why not create your own channel and post updates and content. Add a bit of humor to it, make it a bit graphically appealing and you'll get more hits. Who knows, you might go viral one day!

E-news

First we had a paper newsletter (I even had a 20 page magazine at one point) then we had electronic newsletters. Now a lot of people have forgotten about them. They are super useful. You can send a summary of the week / month to your database of content and happenings. Maybe even some celebrations.

Forum – connecting

You organize gatherings in board rooms, town halls, seminar rooms and the like. What about a gathering on the Internet? What if you created a 'private forum' for your clients only? It could be a place for them to hang out, interact with each other, ask questions about each other

> Quotable quote:
> *"What if you created a 'private forum' for your clients only?"*

and get to know each other. You can do this for free with Facebook and LinkedIn by starting a secret group. Easy peasy to do and no one does it. As humans we like a place of belonging – a place of community. Why not have the Accountant create that for us.

Search Engine Optimization

You can pay for this to get it. And it is not that expensive. Here's how it works. When someone searches for you / what you do / your location or specialty you want to be on the first page of the search engine. It is pointless being on the second page of Google® because the statistics show (by the social media commentators) that if I have to go to the 2nd page then I don't. At least the vast majority of people do not. So you want to engage a company to do this for you and when someone searches under any permutation of searches that may suit what you do then you need to be there – in their face on the first page.

Social Advertising

One of the coolest things about social media advertising has got to be 're-marketing.' This is where if you show interest in a site or style of product when you go elsewhere on the Internet these similar companies appear all of the time. When you're on Facebook, amazingly on the side bar ads appear of things you are interested in. It's because you have been to something similar before and it is 'following you.' Everywhere you go on the Internet a little 'digital footprint' is left. That data is then used to target you and others to buy/visit more of the same. Accountants need to use this in their arsenal.

Other people's blogs

Seeing you are writing why don't you write for others as well? If you have a 'center of influence' that has your target market as their clients then why not offer to write for them. You could be a guest blogger for magazines (where your target market hangs out) and you could offer to blog for industry associations. When you position yourself as an expert and you are writing extensively, people believe you!

Content marketing

Accountants are so scared to give away content / information for free. Why? Is that all you've got? The real value in the content is not the content but the **implementation of the content.** By giving your content away for free (using all the channels in this chapter) you tell me you are confident, you're not scared and I can learn about you before I engage with you. Send me articles, videos, podcasts, white papers, research – anything that builds your credibility. People buy from people they know, like & trust. I may know you by name and I may like you when I meet you. I trust you when I can see what you can do for me.

> Quotable quote:
>
> *"The real value in the content is not the content but the* ***implementation of the content.*** *"*

The Internet is rife with content from dubious sources. Why not give content on what I can do for free. Then sell the how to do it for a lot of money.

We learnt our ABC's as a child. The new ABC is '**Always Be Contributing.**' Not every now and again but every day. The objective is to be seen as a thought leader. If you want to be a thought leader and be 'everywhere' then you need to be everywhere!

Growing your database

If you want to grow your client base then you'll need to massively grow the size of your prospective client database. It's all about getting your target market to enter and 'opt in' to your database. Once they have entered, the objective is to grow your prospective client database into a 'clean' and 'receptive' database. The size of your prospective client database will depend on your marketing capabilities and your growth targets.

Let's say you want to grow your active client base by 26% each year – which means you double the size of your client base every 3 years. It is commonly known in marketing circles that it takes 9 times for a targeted prospect to hear or see a message before they act. The problem is that because of proliferation of marketing messages that we all receive, as consumers we only get to 'see' every 6th message that is sent to us. I call this 'Rob's rule of 54' – 9 times to hear it and only every 6th message sent is seen. Before the turn of this decade I used to call it 'Rob's rule of 27' – 9 times to hear it and 3 times to see it. Our attention spans have reduced by around 50% and we are getting more messaging than ever before. It takes more creativity, more discipline and more patience to get people to respond these days. Based on my theory you need to send up to 54 messages BEFORE you get a response!

> Quotable quote:
>
> *"I call this 'Rob's rule of 54' – 9 times to hear it and only every 6th message sent is seen."*

If that's the case then the size of your prospective client database is a mathematical equation. Based on my equations (verified by a very accurate spreadsheet) then your prospective client database (based on 26% growth pa of client base) needs to be 14 times the size of your current client base. The table below highlights the size your database needs to be based on the volume of clients you want to acquire via marketing methods.

TOTAL CLIENTS	NEW CLIENTS NEEDED PER ANNUM	DATABASE SIZE (54 X NEW CLIENTS)	MULTIPLE OF CURRENT CLIENTS FOR DATABASE SIZE
250	65	3,510	14
315	82	4,423	14
397	103	5,572	14
500	130	7,021	14
630	164	8,847	14
794	206	11,147	14
1000	260	14,045	14

Once you know who you are targeting you can work out where they 'hang out' and target them. You could find out which conferences they attend. What publications they read. Which websites they frequent and so on. With the objective of creating a large list of names that you can market to your 'appearance' (in a variety of forms) where they hang out is crucial to building your list.

Based on your 'privacy act' laws in your country you may be able to buy a list of your target market or you can use a wide variety of techniques to attract your prospective market to your database. One of the best ways to grow your database is to find other non-competing companies (hosts) who have your target market as their current target market and arrange a beneficial marketing campaign. For example you could write a white paper based on your expertise and have the host company email it out so their list can get access to the paper. The prospective client fills in their contact details and now you own the name. There are many other techniques such as 're-marketing,' social media usage, SEO and nurture sequences to attract and create lists. There is so much detail in these that I will save it for another book!

Marketing must generate leads

The overall (and desired) objective of marketing functions in an Accounting firm is to generate leads. Lots of leads. The more marketing you do, the more leads you get, the more choices you have!

There are 2 types of marketing people – brand orientated or direct response. The brand orientated people are vital to your 'look & feel' of your corporate identity. They are vital in helping to build credibility. They will make you look great and you'll feel really good about the work they do. However, they

> Quotable quote:
>
> *"There are 2 types of marketing people – brand orientated or direct response."*

may not get you in front of your target market nor will they enable you to make much money – but you'll look good! My view is that you can outsource a lot of your brand development to contractors or offshore labor. You don't need to have branding types on your payroll.

The type of marketing people (and thus activity) you're looking for is a 'direct response' orientated person. These people are trained differently and your objective with them is to engage your target market and create enquiries for you to follow up. This is NOT the primary role of a Partner. The primary role of a progressive Partner is a sales and nurturing role. Direct response marketing needs to be done by professionals who know what they are doing. It's all about generating leads. The volume of leads you need is determined by your sales conversion rate and your new client (or new services per client) objectives. You can outsource your lead generation, however if you want rapid growth it is far more effective to have the resource(s) in-house.

Your leads are going to come from 2 sources – existing clients or new clients. Both of them are a rich source of new business. The objective is to engage with your client or prospective client and have them respond to you. This is now a lead or an enquiry. Someone who is interested to talk with you further.

If you want someone to respond then you have to give them reasons to respond. And you need to give them a taste of what you have to offer. Just like you when you buy something you like to 'experience' it first. It's no different with Professional Services. How can your current or prospective client experience your smarts before they buy your smarts? Can they download a report, watch a video, listen to a podcast, read an article, attend a seminar or all of the above?

> Quotable quote:
>
> *"How can your current or prospective client experience your smarts before they buy your smarts?"*

The diagram below is an example of 32 methods you could employ to get a response from someone. All of them work. Some of them cost more money, some more time. Some are a more effective use of your money and time, some are more leveraged. All of them work in varying degrees.

MARKETING GRAVITY PLAN

There is not one way to get an enquiry any more. People respond in different ways to different mediums and methods.

Remember the objective is to generate leads (interested people who want to speak with you) and unless you have some decent marketing resource you are not going to be able to employ all 32 strategies. So here are the top 6.

The 6 best ways (time, money and effectiveness) that get a great response are:

No. 10 – Referrals. Every Accountant on the planet knows that a referral from an existing client is the gold standard of new business. An existing client that is happy with you and your firm is 'putting their neck out' to refer someone they know. So you know all this – but are you using it? How many clients do you ask to refer new clients to you? How often do you ask? The key is to start asking! Many firms put out the wrong vibe when

> Quotable quote:
> *"Many firms put out the wrong vibe when it comes to referrals. Clients may ask you how's business and the typical response is 'flat out' or 'busy.'"*

it comes to referrals. Clients may ask you how's business and the typical response is 'flat out' or 'busy.' What have you just told your client? We're too busy for any more business so don't refer! Sometimes your clients can see that you're so busy by the amount of time it takes to get work done. Why would they jeopardize service standards by referring a new client? When you ask for referrals only ask your 'A & B' class clients. Don't ask your 'D' class clients – their friends are idiots as well.

No. 14 – The Internet. I have covered 'web dominance' in this chapter already. If you skipped it or ignored it then here is the summary! The Internet is a rich source of new leads if your site is interactive and interesting enough. It is common habit to 'Google®' everything before we buy it. What does your web presence say about you and your firm? How can I interact with your website? Can I download your position papers? Can I view a video? Does it look modern or is it stuck in the last decade? Is there an enquiry form? Can I fill in a calculator? Can I fill in an online questionnaire and get reports on how my business is going? Can I buy a small product from the site so I can try you out? Is there an up-to-date blog on the site? These are all methods of engagement with your website. If you get engagement you'll get leads.

No. 18 – Workflow. If you have the mindset that in this current job there is a potential another job then you'll never be short of leads. A lead can come from an existing or potential client. Within the current piece of business (let's say compliance) if you have your 'leads radar' on, then there is a good chance you'll find another opportunity that you need to explore. If you are on the lookout for trends or anomalies in the finances then you have a perfect conversation starter (lead) with the client. What most firms who are really good at this are doing is they are spending 20 minutes on every client (when the financials are finished) and brainstorming what else they could do for this client. Of course, do not make the mistake that some do and just do this work for the client. It is a separate engagement.

No. 19 – Alliance Development. If you know what your ideal client looks like (your best buyer) then you can easily find other non-competing businesses / organizations that have your best client as their client or member. Once you know who your potential alliance is now it's time to nurture them and ask them for referrals. You will need to pitch your business and your offering to them

> Quotable quote:
>
> *"Many firms I know will run joint seminars with their referral sources and offer free reports & white papers to their client / member base."*

and give them reason to refer their clients to you. Many firms I know will run joint seminars with their referral sources and offer free reports and white papers to their client / member base. If you come from the position of adding value first and helping your alliance out with new value for their market, then they will refer. If you try to first sell to them or their clients you'll put them on the back foot and they may not refer.

No. 27 – Webinars. If you have a large database and they are educated to web based events (you can educate them) then you can run your own webinar. A webinar is simply a seminar over the web. You might schedule a webinar for 60 minutes at an appropriate time that suits your target market. You could prepare a PowerPoint presentation and deliver it. You could interview 2 or 3 of your successful clients about your topic. You could offer a free consultation or report at the end. The reason I like webinars is because they are quick, cheap and effective in generating leads. You get amazing leverage by sitting in your office talking to (possibly) hundreds of people at a time.

No. 31 – Seminars. Without a doubt the best way to introduce new services to your clients is by running seminars of some sort. However they are expensive to run. The event could be a large scale business seminar, a private boardroom briefing, a small workshop or similar. You can certainly meet with your clients 'one on one' but that is quite slow. When running seminars you need to offer some value – not just selling. The best attended seminars are where the business owner can take away ideas they can apply right away. That might include: cash flow management, KPI reporting, profit improvement or revenue growth. Start with a short 2 hour event that includes a 'demo' of the new system (let's say a cloud accounting program) and Q&A.

No matter what methods you employ you need to measure the effectiveness. Remember this is direct response marketing so everything should be measured. If you do not measure the effectiveness of your marketing then pretty quickly you will get despondent with the time and expense that goes into it.

> Quotable quote:
>
> *"If you do not measure the effectiveness of your marketing then pretty quickly you will get despondent with the time and expense that goes into it."*

An example of measuring is below:

ACTIVITY	TARGET	QUANTITY	COST	SEND DATE	RESPONSE %	RESPONSE #	GROSS PROFIT	ROI
Letter #1	Existing clients	463	$565	Dec 15	3.35%	15	$2,085	369%
Letter #2	Suspect list	3,323	$4,500	Dec 15	1.25%	41	$5,699	126%
Email #1	Existing Clients	463	$4.63	Dec 17	1%	5	$695	15000%
Webinar #1	Entire database	92	$50	Jan 15	12%	11	$1,529	3058%
Email #2	Suspect list	3,323	$33.23	Jan 18	0.5%	16	$2,224	6690%
Fax #1	Suspect list	3,323	$2,500	Feb 1	2.1%	67	$9,313	372%
Telemarketing Test	Suspect sample	500	$3,500	Feb 5	4.5%	22	$3,058	87%

You can see that the campaigns are measured down to the decimal point. Everything should be based on a return on investment and any marketing and sales activity that you do should be treated as an investment.

Let's say you're looking to acquire new clients. If you were buying a fee base from another firm then in most parts around the world you would gladly spend 75 cents to $1 for every dollar of new clients. You know that you will keep the client for 10 plus years so you get your money back from year 2 onwards.

The same applies to marketing and sales. If you do a marketing campaign and it costs you $10,000 and you generate 3 hot leads and that results in 2 new clients worth $7,500 each, then provided your cashflow can sustain it you would keep doing the campaign.

I think every firm needs to have what's called an *'allowable acquisition cost'* and an *'allowable lead cost'* for new clients. It means you are prepared to spend up to $X to get the client for the first time. The way you work it out is based on your gross profit of your target client and when you want to get a return on your investment.

A simple example is this. Let's say your target client has an annual fee of $10,000 and the gross profit on every new client is $6,000 per annum. If you had an allowable acquisition cost of $3,000 then you make your money back in 6 months. Now unless you are a sales superstar you are not going to convert every lead. Let's say you meet with all leads and convert 1 in 3. That means your allowable lead cost could be $1,000. So now you give a budget to your marketing team of no more than $1,000 spent per quality lead. Based on your current sales skills it will take you 3 leads to get a sale and therefore the cost of acquisition is $3,000. Rinse & repeat.

Do not think of marketing and sales costs as a percentage of revenue or a fixed amount per year. You'll limit your potential. When you think of marketing and sales as an investment that is measured then you have an almost endless budget – effectiveness, monitoring and cashflow dependent.

To Remain Relevant you must make lots of and lots of targeted noise!

> Quotable quote:
>
> *"I think every firm needs to have what's called an* **'allowable acquisition cost'** *and an* **'allowable lead cost'** *for new clients."*

> Quotable quote:
>
> *"Do not think of marketing and sales costs as a percentage of revenue or a fixed amount per year."*

Chapter 8

Noise without follow up is just noise

Sales is a confidence game

There's an old saying that dogs can smell fear. It's the same theory for people who are in a sales role. If your 'dog' (person in front of you) can sense that you are not confident then you are not going to make the sale. You will get questions and objections from the prospect/client that you don't want and ultimately not make the sale.

Just the thought of the word 'sales' can put the heeby jeebies into Accountants. For some reason Accountants don't like the word. I am unsure why that is. Maybe they think it's a bit 'grubby' and 'we don't sell – we're professionals.' Do you think new business will just come to you because you are a professional? Yes, you are a professional. You're a professional that needs to learn how to sell otherwise you're not going to thrive. To remain relevant in the future you must learn the art of sales. Accountants are really good at sales (once you're taught) because you come from a position of trust and authority. The credibility is already there before you open your mouth and start talking.

If you don't like the word 'sales' then how about changing your mindset to 'servicing your clients properly.' The duty of care that an Accountant has with their client is that if you spot an issue or an opportunity then you are obliged to let the client know about it. It's in your

> Quotable quote:
>
> *"If you don't like the word 'sales' then how about changing your mindset to 'servicing your clients properly.'"*

code of conduct if I am not mistaken. As you dig deeper into this and if you are super interested in your clients, then **all clients should be buying everything they need from you that helps them achieve their goals.** That means you need to service them properly – aka making SALES and helping them to buy.

Every Accountant is involved in sales in every client interaction. Making a sale is a transfer of trust. Even when you are recommending a type of structure or a tax plan you are selling. You are taking your idea and convincing the client that they need to use it or buy it. You do it every day when you meet with a client. You are selling every day. Accounting is selling.

Back to the dogs and the fear. No matter what techniques, process or questions you adopt in your sales role, it is all a waste of time unless you have confidence in what you are doing or promoting. To be good at sales and good at transferring trust every Accountant needs to work on their confidence levels. The more confidence you have the more successful you'll be.

> Quotable quote:
> *"To be good at sales and good at transferring trust every Accountant needs to work on their confidence levels."*

To increase your confidence levels I think there are 8 areas to work on:

1. Language
2. Tonality
3. Health
4. Dress
5. Knowledge
6. Success
7. Stories
8. Process

Language. What you say is so important while you are communicating with prospects and clients. It's the language of the sale.

Do you ask open ended questions or closed questions? Closed questions get a yes/no/maybe answer – e.g.: Do you have a will? Open ended questions get a detailed response. E.g.: What is your documented plan for your loved ones when you are gone?

Are you telling your prospect/client what they need or are your explaining why they need it? E.g.: You need a budget and cashflow forecast vs. Our best clients are freeing up new cashflow and creating more profit by having a detailed and real time budget and cashflow forecast.

Are you giving statements or articulating your value and ending with a question? E.g.: You need to apply our tax strategies so you can save some tax this year. Or... We've worked out you'll save $40,000 per year for the next 10 years if you apply our tax strategies. That's a minimum of $400,000 that we can help you with. I'm curious, what would you do with $40,000 per year that you don't have to pay?

Learning the language of the sale will give you more confidence and more importantly your prospect or client will see the confidence in you.

> Quotable quote:
>
> *"Learning the language of the sale will give you more confidence and more importantly your prospect or client."*

Tonality. Not only is it what you say it's also how you say it. When you are in a conversation are you boring and monotone or do you have a bit of passion in your voice? Are you miserable looking or do you smile? Do you sit still or do you point and wave your hands? Do you alter your volume (higher and lower) during conversation or do you remain flat? Do you talk faster sometimes and slower at other times to make a point?

You're supposed to be transferring passion in a sales environment. When I am in your presence can I feel the passion and the excitement? If you want me to transfer funds to you I need to know that you're excited by the idea that you're selling.

> Quotable quote:
>
> *"When I am in your presence can I feel the passion and the excitement?"*

Whenever I design a seminar, I write a 'running sheet' which is how the day will run. I have it timed in 5 minute blocks so I am covering key content at certain times. I never rehearse and I am always on time. I live by my running sheet. At the top of every running sheet I have my ENERGY objective, my personal

STATE and my business OBJECTIVE. Here is the top of a recent running sheet.

Capitalizing on the Cloud – Running Sheet

E*nergy.* To create an inspiring, challenging, environment for Accountants to realize their potential. The program will be full of energy, passion, excitement and practical strategies.
State: Give it everything – Excited, Thankful, Privilege, Humble, Sharing, Fun, Best ever, Smiling all the time
Objective: Influence the delegates to take action

The top of the running sheet sets my tonality for the program. I have it on me at all times. My team has a copy as well. Even if I am tired, I want to set the tone and put on a great program.

The tonality of you will have a big impact on your confidence.

Health. It's a known fact that when you are fitter, stronger and healthier you feel better about yourself. Your health could mean your body weight, your bad teeth, your hair loss, your fitness level or even your skin complexion. All can be fixed. I don't think Accountants need to train excessively to run marathons or compete in triathlons to get more confidence. However, if that's your thing then go for it.

You may only need to lose enough weight for people to notice and pay you a compliment. Or you just getting your teeth professionally cleaned or adjusted might help you to smile more. You might need to see a dermatologist to get your skin seen to or a hair loss specialist to see what you can do with your receding hairline. Even training moderately a few times a week can improve your health and fitness.

> Quotable quote:
>
> *"Even training moderately a few times a week can improve your health and fitness."*

I remember once talking to the Partners of a 3 partner firm. They were complaining that there was no energy in the office and everyone was pretty 'steady.' They wanted a better culture with more energy in the office. They asked for my advice so I gave it to them. I was in one of my 'blunt' moods so I simply said to them:

"Look, a fish rots from the head down. How will there ever be more energy in the business while the 3 of you are unfit and overweight?"

They got the message. They went on a health kick, lost some pounds and lead from the front. Your health makes a big difference to your confidence levels. Maybe it's time to sharpen up.

Dress. Look sharp and be sharp. Most Accountants (hopefully not you) I get to meet are 'cheap' so they buy cheap shoes, wear cheap suits and use cheap tools. The way you dress says so much about you and your style. If you look sloppy then typically your work will be sloppy. If you use a cheap pen and paper then I wonder about the quality of what you are telling me. If you wear ill-fitting cheap suits and out of date clothing does that mean you are out of date as well?

I am not saying that you need to spend $2,000+ on a big brand suit. However a decent suit that is properly adjusted to your body shape does make a difference. I am suggesting you ditch the cheap conference pen you got for free and the $2 notepad to something more upmarket. You are taking notes about my business and my future – please pay me some respect by using decent tools. You are offering me business advice and you look disheveled – it doesn't instill confidence in me.

If you are having problems with matching clothing then hire a stylist for the day to take you shopping. For the sake of the fashion police get rid of the 1990's look and get up to date. Your confidence will improve as a result.

> Quotable quote:
>
> *"If you are having problems with matching clothing then hire a stylist for the day to take you shopping."*

Knowledge. Knowledge is an interesting one and some Accountants take it too far and want to know everything about a subject before they can talk about it. You don't need to know everything about a topic to know a lot. You just need to get good at asking questions and letting the other person talk. The idea of knowledge is to get more out of it and become more knowledgeable. It's about broadening your knowledge base so you are more interesting to talk to. The more interesting you are to talk with the more sales you'll make.

I am amazed at how many Accountants do not read the national financial newspapers at least 3 times per week. You're in the finance industry yet you don't read the finance news. Bizarre! You don't have to read the newspaper from cover to cover just scan the main headlines. You can store that content for later and if needed pull it out in conversation. The Internet is a wonderful tool for getting useful knowledge – sporting scores, political movements, the latest IPO, trade news, etc.

It's all about becoming a better conversationalist. If you become a better conversationalist you'll be more relatable and you get more confidence.

> Quotable quote:
> "If you become a better conversationalist you'll be more relatable and you get more confidence."

Success. The inner confidence of knowing that the work you do is really good shines through in your conversations. Every Accountant I have ever met (over 100,000 so far) has done some great work for clients. You have saved clients tax, improved their cashflow, kept them out of jail, been a shoulder to cry on, improved their profit and even helped some to be very wealthy.

What are you doing with all that success you have created? How many testimonials and case studies have you collected? In my business we have the 'wall of fame.' As we meet a client for the first time we take a photo of them, print it in black & white and then get them to write something nice on it. I got the idea from the old school restaurants where the 'celebrity' signed their photograph and wrote something nice to the restaurateur. We've filled one wall and have started 2 more. So far there are around 1,200 photographs of happy clients and loads of positive words. The main wall of fame is in the hallway on the way to the restrooms. As you go to do your business you feel better about business!

We also have a big focus on W.H.A.M's – Written Happy Accountants Moments. When we interact with our clients we ask them to put something in writing on what they are experiencing when using our services and tools. In 10 weeks flat we once collected 102 of them. From there we go back and create proper case studies.

As the old saying goes 'success breeds success.' Documenting the success of your clients gives you more confidence and also your team.

Stories. Telling stories is so important in a sales conversation. It's all about instilling social proof in me. I am sitting in front of you and you are espousing to the fact that I need to do something different. I trust you and respect you but

> Quotable quote:
>
> *"Telling a relevant story can give me that social proof I am looking for."*

deep down I am wondering if you can actually do what you say you can do. Telling a relevant story can give me that social proof I am looking for. Here are a couple of examples:

> *"The situation you are in is so close to another manufacturing client we helped last year. They had rising costs, did about the same amount of revenue as you and were faced with new competitors who drove the product price down. This caused a cashflow issue and pressure from their bank. What we did for them was to put in place a budget and cashflow forecast, helped them to re-finance their debt and we worked with them every month to monitor their cashflow. After 6 months they could see the difference and after 12 months they had excess cashflow because we financially coached them out of the problem."*

> *"I understand how you must be feeling right now. When we have had this conversation regarding re-structuring company affairs most of the clients we have done this with felt exactly the same way you do right now – annoyed and anxious. One client in particular was annoyed with their previous Accountant because he wasn't struc-tured correctly. He was anxious as to how the family might take the new changes that we recommended. What he found was that when we showed him he was financially better off for making the changes he jumped at the opportunity."*

Telling stories gives social proof and it instills confidence in the person you are sitting with that you know what you're talking about.

> Quotable quote:
>
> *"Telling stories gives social proof and it instills confidence in the person you are sitting with that you know what you're talking about."*

Process. If you are like most modern firms you will have an office procedures manual. That manual is all about how you do tasks in the office. They typically have guidelines, checklists, a process and standard letters. Someone at some time worked out the best way to file, scan, copy, collect the mail, lock up the office and pay the salaries. Then it was documented so others could follow the steps.

Sales is just like that. A sales process is like a workflow process. One thing triggers the next thing until a resolution happens. There is always someone in the office that is the best at sales. Hopefully they have been trained by my company! If they are good then sit with them and document their process. What do they do at each step of the way? What do they say? How do they say it? What's their process flow? Once the process is worked out it needs to be documented into a sales manual. The sales manual includes the sales process and the document is called a 'Playbook'. It's the game plan of how you want to play to win.

The objective is to create a repeatable sales process. A repeatable sales process will give you more confidence. More confidence leads to high self-belief. High self-belief leads to more sales. The dogs can smell it.

Question away

I am blessed to be working with the Accounting profession for 20+ years. I love the influence that you can make and the difference to a client's financial position. You are very loyal to your clients, your vendors and your team. You are sometimes obstinate on parting with money but that is not the most annoying thing. The most annoying thing in dealing with you, is that you don't ask enough questions. Sometimes none at all. It is so frustrating.

I am unsure why you don't ask questions. I am unsure why you are not more curious. I have a feeling that you think you need to know the answers and that asking questions is a sign of weakness. Quite the opposite. It's like you want to give the answers all the time rather than coax the answer out by asking quality questions.

The challenge with this behavior in a sales situation is that you jump to conclusions too fast and you do not unearth the real issues or opportunities. You end up talking more than your client and you are prescribing too fast without enough diagnosis. You have to remember to ZIP IT in a sales situation and not give the answer right away.

> Quotable quote:
>
> *"You have to remember to ZIP IT in a sales situation and not give the answer right away."*

You have to ask quality questions in a structured way without giving away the answers. To simplify the types of questions to ask you just need to remember BPOMVCT. You need to be asking questions to establish the situation and understand the **background**. You

> Quotable quote:
>
> *"Your prospect needs to tell you the **value** proposition when they implement your suggestions."*

need to dig deep to find all of the **problems**. You need to understand the short and long term **objectives**. You need to establish the **measurement** metrics. Your prospect needs to tell you the **value** proposition when they implement your suggestions. Your prospect needs to understand the **consequences** of not doing something different. You both need to establish the **timing** of getting started.

Asking questions with confidence and truly listening is the absolute best way to get sales. But it is absolutely pointless unless you LISTEN.

The way you ask questions is just as important as the question itself. Here are some simple question asking tips:

1. **Conversational NOT Interrogational.** Not rapid fire, pause and listen.
2. **Use question softeners.** The softener proceeds the question - E.g. So that I can help you best…. could I just ask…. that's interesting, have you….
3. **Answer a question with another question.** E.g. Yes, we can do that, tell me what else are you looking for help in?

4. **Give positive strokes.** It shows you are listening. E.g. Ahh ha, I see, Really, I understand, Tell me more about that.
5. **Feedback what the client says.** E.g. So what you are saying is…. So you said your objectives are….
6. **Always be confirming.** E.g. Just to confirm… OK, to confirm you are ….

As you go into a meeting with a prospect or a client you should be ready to ask some great questions. Here are 17 killer questions you can have in your tool box and pull out when needed.

1. I am curious. You started this business 10 years ago. When you started it where did you think you would be today?
2. What's been the progress of your revenue and profit for the last 3 years?
3. What are some of the best decisions you have made in the last 3 years?
4. What are some of the worst decisions you have made in the last 3 years?
5. How many customers do you have?
6. How many times do they buy from you?
7. What is the approximate average transaction value?
8. If you could wave a magic wand what would be some of the problems you have in business that you would like to go away?
9. Let's look at the next 5 years – where would you like to be with your wealth creation?
10. What would it mean to you if we could help you achieve your objectives?
11. How would you know if we have helped you get there?
12. How would you handle the volume of sales that might come from our work with you?
13. What's your plan B?
14. What are the consequences of not doing something different?
15. We are really good at fixing what you have explained. How would you like us to help you?
16. What's stopping you from getting started right now?
17. What is your decision making process?

Do not ask dumb questions like '*what keeps you awake at night?*' It is so stupid to ask that one. You're going to get answers like – snoring, baby, the train, loud music – rather than what you are looking for.

You want to ask questions that invoke a response and help you move closer to a YES. When you look at human behavior we buy professional services for only 5 (or a mix of) reasons:

1. To make money
2. To save money
3. To save time
4. To achieve pleasure
5. To fix pain

Your products and services can help in most of those areas. You just need to find out what is most important to them right now. You could ask the following question to flush out the highest motivation right now:

"Our work with business owners like yourself is focused on 5 key areas. We are helping our clients to 1) grow revenue and wealth 2) dramatically increase profit 3) minimize tax 4) protect assets and 5) improve cashflow. Which of those are most important to you right now?"

Then let them talk. You are flushing out the core objectives at the outset by asking questions like this. People typically buy additional services from Accountants to move away from something (pain related) or move towards something (pleasure related).

It's human nature that people will tend to buy more to solve pain than to achieve pleasure. The pain in a business could be:

1. Cashflow related
2. People related
3. Client service
4. Losing revenue

5. Profitability related
6. Competitor related

When the level of *'pissedoffness'* (technical term for really annoyed) is high they will buy. You need to find that pain in the conversations you have with your clients or prospects. When you find the pain, you then exacerbate the pain (powerful sales technique here) by asking more questions about the painful area. You keep asking and probing and provoking the pain area. You *'poke the bruise'* until it hurts.

> Quotable quote:
> *"When the level of **'pissedoffness'** (technical term for really annoyed) is high they will buy."*

Based on my observation of thousands of sales meetings the decision to buy or not can be broken down to the following:

*   50% of the decision is based on their reasons why, their objectives, their motivation and the benefits the solution will offer them.
*   40% of the decision is based on the credibility of the seller, the relationship with the seller, the trust of the seller and the likeability of the seller.
*   10% of the decision is based on the product, the process, the content or the methodology.

Make sure you spend 90% of your time on them and only 10% on what you can do for them. You will increase your credibility and trust as you ask more and more questions.

As you go through your sales meetings you're ultimately looking for a resolution to the conversation. There are only 3 final answers in a sales process – YES, NO or NOT NOW. You might get a MAYBE from time to time but that is typically a smoke screen for an objection.

If you get a maybe then you have not found out the pain points enough. You

> Quotable quote:
> *"Asking quality open ended questions are at the heart of a sales conversation."*

haven't found out the true objectives.

Asking quality open ended questions are at the heart of a sales conversation. To remain relevant in the future you're going to need to get good at sales. Asking questions will help you get there. Go ahead – ask me one!

Sales systems

I have been actively selling something since the age of 14. That's 30+ years of selling. I have been formally trained in courses on how to sell. I have attended more sales seminars than I care to remember. I have read countless books and listened to audio programs on the science of sales. I have sold over the phone, on the shop floor in retail, from a seminar stage, one on one, one to many and via webinars.

I have always been good at sales because I use some simple systems that I have learned and fine-tuned to keep me on track.

I have never shared some of these systems before to anyone except my own sales team. Seeing this is a book of valuable content I thought you might like some of the 'secret sauce' of my selling systems.

Sales System # 1 – Getting through to the owners

Owners of businesses are busy people. They are our buyer(s) and they are the ones (and the only ones) you need to speak with. If you do a sales meeting with anyone but the ultimate decision maker(s) then expect to do the meeting again. But you have to get through to them to start the conversation and build the relationship.

> Quotable quote:
>
> "If you do a sales meeting with anyone but the ultimate decision maker(s) then expect to do the meeting again."

I find that using the concept of a pre-booked telephone meeting will help enormously. I remember sitting in an airport lounge once where I made 26 telephone meetings (via reception) in the space of 1 hour. I simply smashed

> Quotable quote:
>
> "I find that using the concept of a pre-booked telephone meeting will help enormously."

the phone, booked the meetings and then sent them individual confirmation notes later.

If your target owner has communicated with you somehow via a marketing report download, a seminar or has made an enquiry of some sort then it should be easy to get through. But you don't necessarily want to speak to the owner right away. You might need 15 minutes and if you randomly call you may only get 3.

Your script goes like this:

> *"Hi Mary (person who answers phone), it's John James calling from XYZ firm, Bob was on our website and he downloaded a free report we offered and I wanted to catch up with him to discuss it further - but not right now. What I'd like to do is find 15 minutes that works for both of us and I'll call him at that time. Do you have access to his diary so we can schedule the phone appointment?"*

OR if you get through to Bob right away.

> *"Hi Bob, its John James calling from XYZ firm, I wanted to catch up with you for 15 minutes on the phone - but not right now. What I would like to do is book a telephone meeting with you to discuss how we can help you improve your cashflow and grow your revenue. Have you got your schedule handy so we can book a time over the next week or so?"*

Rob's rules of telephone meetings;

1. Use an odd time - say 1010, 0915, 0920, 1125
2. Send an email to prospect stating the meeting time
3. Always call out - do not let them call you - EVER
4. Always call PRECISELY on time - watch the second hand before you dial
5. Always announce yourself to reception "Bob and I have a pre-booked phone appointment at 9:15am which is now, can you put me through, please"
6. If Bob is not available then ***do not let him call you back.*** Simply state "that's OK, I've got a pretty tight schedule like Bob, can we re-schedule and I will call again then?"

7.   Never leave a message for someone to call you back. It's lazy sales and invariably if they do call you back then it'll be at the wrong time.

Sales System # 2 – Meeting worksheet

Most Accountants I have met use an interview pad of some sort in meetings. It'll have space for the client details at the top and then typically it will have blank ruled lines for note taking. The really good sales people I know are prepared for the meeting with a process flow of how the meeting will work. The really, really good ones will take that process flow and make it the interview pad. That way you always remember your process flow and get to the conclusion you want faster. Here is an example of an interview pad that you could R&D!

> Quotable quote:
>
> *"The really good sales people I know are prepared for the meeting with a process flow of how the meeting will work."*

Sensational meeting, positive, listening, understanding		My state of mind
		Client name / business type
		Why here, set the scene
		Who are the buyers? – (decision making questions - DQ's)
$	Revenue	Situation & background – (background related questions - BQ's)
$	Profit	
$	Debt	
$	Cash assets	
	Age	
	Kids + ages	
	Business progress	
	Goals when started business:	

	3 – 5 years out	Objectives & motivation – the Awesome 8: growth, profit, cashflow, asset protection, tax minimization, succession, retirement, estate planning – (Motivation related questions - MQ's)
	Earnings goal in retirement	
	Retirement age	
	Lifestyle goals	
	Time / hobbies	
$	Size of problem $M	
$	Overdraft / Cash	Objectives & problems in the way – (problem related questions - PQ's)
	Time issues	
	People issues	
		Measures – how will you know if achieved – (Measurement metrics questions MMQ's)
		Value – assuming achieved, what would that mean to you and your family? – (Value related questions – VQ's)
	Consequences of not doing	Timing – assuming paid for out of new cashflow – (Consequence and timing questions CQ's & TQ's)
	Getting started – cyclical issues?	
Go away and think about it – send implementation plan		Options
Proposal, read, meet questions, start date		BAMFAM (book a meeting from a meeting)

Sales System # 3 – Sales nurturing system

Your prospects are busy people. They have demands on their time every day and most days they have sales people attempt to sell to them every day. You are competing against a lot of noise, interruptions and constant bombardment of information. Although the prospect may have met you, downloaded a report from your website or even attended one of your seminars – **assume they have forgotten who you are.** To get them to remember you in between calls you need to be memorable. The way to do that is with a nurturing system that happens immediately after the first contact and does not end until they buy or die! Here's how it works.

What	When	Method
Phone	On the first call	Find some personal information about the prospect
Mail	Immediately after 1st contact	Send handwritten thank you card + business card included
Email	Immediately after 1st contact	Confirm next meeting details with PA/reception and prospect
Social tools	Immediately after 1st contact	Connect to prospect by LinkedIn, Facebook and Twitter
Phone	2 days before next meeting	Confirm meeting details
Email	Monthly	Re-forward with personal note (not sure if you have seen this) every Newsletter you send to your existing clients
Email	As new videos loaded	Send out a link to any new video on YouTube channel
Email	As new reports are loaded	Send out a link to any new white paper / report (not sure if you have seen this...)
Mail	1 week after first contact	Send handwritten card with something of interest (magazine or article what they are interested in)
Mail	On birthday	Send birthday card
Email	As they are created	Send case studies (not sure if you have seen this or not, give me a call if you need some help) every time they are produced

Sales System # 4 - Return on Investment (ROI) based selling

ROI based selling is when you establish a starting point with a current financial model and then plan the future by altering the base numbers that are input based numbers. Then your solution is the answer to helping them achieve the result.

An example would be to use the growth equation in PANALITIX (**www.panalitix.com**) to sell to them. Or using the Business Strategy Map (send me an

> Quotable quote:
>
> *"ROI based selling is when you establish a starting point with a current financial model and then plan the future by altering the base numbers that are input based numbers."*

email and I'll send you a free copy) and altering the numbers. Or you could simply use a white board, flip chart or a conversation.

You can use ROI based selling in situations such as:

- Revenue improvement - key drivers being client numbers, transaction frequency and average transaction value
- Profit improvement - key drivers being revenue, costs and efficiency (AHR, Write ons)
- Cash Flow improvement - key drivers being profit, inventory and receivables

Example - revenue & cash improvement:

Improvement	New numbers	As nominated by your prospect	Base numbers now	Key area
	330	10% increase	300	No. of customers
	4.4	10% increase	4	No. of transactions per customer / year
	$1,650	10% increase	$1,500	Average transaction value
$595,800 revenue improvement	$2,395,800		$1,800,000	Total revenue
	$135,000	40% decrease	$225,000	Inventory balance
	$138,750	25% decrease	$185,000	Accounts receivable balance
$136,250 cash	$273,750		$410,000	Total "Lock Up"

The key to ROI based selling is to get the prospect to volunteer the numbers now and the numbers of improvement.

Sales systems like these will help you enormously in your ultimate pursuit which is to make sure every client is buying every service they need that helps them achieve their goals.

Sales is like workflow management

Most Accountants have a workflow system of sorts. You get the information in, you check the information, you manipulate the information, you query it, and you then bind it up and lodge or file it. It's a process (simplified, I know) that is like a manufacturing line. The raw materials come in and after a series of steps and people touching the item a finished product is created and shipped to the customer.

A sale to a prospect / client in an Accounting firm is exactly like a manufacturing line as well. It's just like workflow management. First of all branding occurs, then lead generation, then contact management, data collection, a series of meetings, a follow-up process and finally after a sale is made, delivery of the sold service. Or to simplify that there are 4 core steps:

> Quotable quote:
>
> *"A sale to a prospect / client in an Accounting firm is exactly like a manufacturing line as well. It's just like workflow management."*

1. Lead generation
2. Lead management
3. Selling
4. Delivery

They happen in that order and there are many strategies, methods and techniques that you could implement to improve each one. The diagram below highlights many of those strategies.

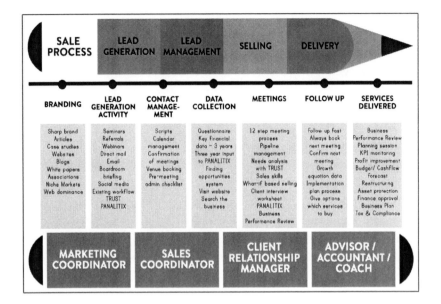

Just like you have different people in workflow scenarios 'touching' the project, you also have different people in a sales process. Your marketing coordinator has different skills to your sales coordinator and your client relationship manager (typically Partners or seniors) needs to allocate time to sales, otherwise it just won't happen. You need to look at this diagram and see where you can improve. If you have a sales machine in action then you should be receiving new leads every day that you can sell to.

Just like you keep an eye on various indicators like utilization / productivity, turnaround time and realization / write-offs for workflow management you also measure different key performance indicators (KPI's) in your sales process. Some sales KPI's to monitor:

- ✓ Database size
- ✓ Open rate and click through rate on campaigns
- ✓ Leads per week / month
- ✓ Follow-up time (hours) from lead created to first contact
- ✓ Number of sales meetings per month per Partner
- ✓ Number of open opportunities per Partner
- ✓ Probability & value of sale

- ✓ Close dates of sale
- ✓ Days to close a sale – from lead to resolution
- ✓ Conversion rate of meetings to sale
- ✓ Average Hourly Rate on the new sale
- ✓ Number of follow-up meetings needed per sale
- ✓ Total selling time per sale

Your objective is to monitor the right numbers, make alterations to your methods and ultimately optimize your sales process. All of this can be monitored and measured through cloud based Customer Relationship Management 'CRM' systems. Your new CRM system (send me an email and I'll send you some links to good ones that other Accountants are using for as little as $25 per month per person) can track your entire pipeline, all of the probability and all of the sales stages. You should be able to create a sales funnel that looks something like the one below so you can see where all prospects are at any given time in the sales cycle.

> Quotable quote:
>
> *"Your objective is to monitor the right numbers, make alterations to your methods and ultimately optimize your sales process."*

OPPORTUNITY / PIPELINE MANAGEMENT

It's called pipeline management or opportunity management. With accurate stages and probability you should be able to forecast your upcoming sales quite accurately. Sales do not happen sitting behind a computer screen all day. You need to get out from behind the desk and meet some people. It's like a wheel barrow. Unless you push it, it won't move.

Many Accountants are employing marketing companies and internal people to generate leads. They're making noise in the marketplace. Without sales follow up it's just noise and a complete waste of time.

Chapter 9
It's a business that makes money

Improving the profit of your Accounting business

The purpose of any business is to find and keep customers. So you have a marketing and sales function to find them and then you have great service and services that 'WOWs' them into staying with you.

That's all well and good for your clients. What about you? You've taken a risk to start / buy your business (it's not a practice and you need to stop practicing – you've been practicing long enough) and you need to be rewarded. In my opinion you need to be rewarded very well for your intellect, your contribution and your risk. I think the benchmark is >$1M profit per Partner with Partners doing minimal client work. Unfortunately the average Partner makes around 1/3 of that number.

Now you may be comfortable with your current number and that may be OK for now. The problem with comfort is that you stop seeking, striving, developing and then apathy tends to kick in. You need a healthy discontent for the present to change. The output of change is profit and cash.

> Quotable quote:
>
> *"The problem with comfort is that you stop seeking, striving, developing and then apathy tends to kick in."*

Here's a dialogue between my son Hugh (when he was 6) and me.

Me: Hugh, it's time to teach you about profit.
Hugh: Dad, what's profit?

Me: It's the selling price minus the buying price. (equation on the whiteboard)

Hugh: Oh, sell take off buy.

Me: Yes, mate, the profit is the result of sales minus costs.

Hugh: Oh.

Me: Hugh, what's profit?

Hugh: Profit is GOOD!

Me: Hugh, how much profit should we make?

Hugh: Hmmm – as much as possible.

You've gotta love young capitalism. Instill it into them young, I say. We still talk about that conversation all these years later (at the time of writing he's 19) and in business it's a very important part of life.

The 6-year-old kid got it. Do you?

Sadly, the Accounting profession seems scared to talk about their own profit and money. Why I ask. It's not a dirty word – it's a healthy word. A healthy vibrant business makes lots of it. A driven business owner makes decisions to get more of it.

And here's the kicker. If you are supposed to be a leader of business then why are you not making more money than your clients? I think you should be making more than ALL OF THEM WHO YOU ADVISE ON BUSINESS MATTERS?

> Quotable quote:
>
> *"If you are supposed to be a leader of business then why are you not making more money than your clients?"*

Ok, rant over. You get my message. I think you deserve more profit and you have the business vehicle to do it. But to maximize the profit you have to change your business model.

Here's how you increase the profit of an Accounting firm. There are 8 primary ways...

> Quotable quote:
>
> *"I think you deserve more profit and you have the business vehicle to do it."*

1. Your mindset and culture
2. Your pricing structure
3. Your cost structure

4. Your efficiency model
5. Your number (& type) of clients
6. Your services
7. Your clients buying more services
8. Your leverage

Your mindset and culture

I have heard it time and time again, 'we're not motivated by more money' or similar trite answers. It's a rubbish answer. There is not a business owner on the planet that if they were handed an extra $1M in income they wouldn't take it. I don't care if you give it away to charity or your kids or waste it at the casino. Either way it'll make you feel better. I understand that you don't promote the fact to your clients that you want to make more profit but I do think you need a profit-driven mindset within you and your team. That means you are always looking for cost saving ideas, new revenue and better pricing methods. You are always looking for ways to sell something new to clients (only if they need it) and always looking for new clients.

According to the 6-year-old, profit is good and you should make as much as possible!

Your pricing structure

Here is the best pricing advice I can give you.
STOP PRICING BY THE HOUR!
Seriously, it'll keep you in the poorhouse and the overworked house. It's a really dumb way to price anything. It assumes the hourly rate was correct and the time to do it was correct. Neither are ever close to being correct. The worst model is when you price based on time taken X hourly rate AFTER the work

> Quotable quote:
> *"Here is the best pricing advice I can give you. STOP PRICING BY THE HOUR!"*

has been done. This model causes inefficiencies, waste, padding of time sheets, go slow mentality and other nasty behaviors. What if you priced every job upfront with a 15% increase on last year? And please don't write it off. What if you assessed your value contribution to the project and priced (in advance) on your value and then worked as hard as you can to deliver the project in the least amount of time possible whilst maintaining quality control?

According to the 6-year-old, profit is good and you should make as much as possible!

Your cost structure

Many firms we work with are seriously looking at (or have already implemented) offshoring with their business. The biggest cost in any Accounting firm is how much you pay for labor. There are not many savings to be made in an Accounting firm other than labor. When you can hire 5-year qualified CPA's in the Philippines for $5 per hour it does make it very tempting to at least explore the opportunity. If you have Accountants in your office who spend most of their time processing work and doing administration (which means they are not really adding value to the client) then you can get that done elsewhere for 4 times less cost. The Accounting firm of the future is one that has a local client facing team and everything else is done somewhere else in a more cost effective location.

> Quotable quote:
> *"The Accounting firm of the future is one that has a local client facing team and everything else is done somewhere else in a more cost effective location."*

According to the 6-year-old, profit is good and you should make as much as possible!

Your efficiency model

There is so much wastage and inefficiencies in an Accounting firm it's not funny. Think of the volume of hours it takes to 'check' client data or the enormous amount of time it takes to get all of 'the missing information' from a client. The human brain can go so much faster if it is under pressure. People can type faster than they currently can if they are trained properly. Accountants spend much of their day doing 'administration tasks associated with the accounting job' instead of doing accounting work. Why not do an overhaul on your systems and the way you interact with clients so you are more efficient. Why not move all your clients across to a cloud accounting system so you can be more efficient. Why not hire professional administrators to do the administration work so you can be more efficient. A word of caution: unless you price jobs upfront, your price will go down with your efficiencies or you'll end up doing more work for the same amount of money.

According to the 6-year-old, profit is good and you should make as much as possible!

Your number (& type) of clients

So you want to improve profit. To do that someone has to pay for your services. Enter your clients. Every Accounting firm I have ever trained, coached or even spoken to has clients who are costing the firm money. They won't change, they are disruptive, they are disorganized and they waste Accountants' time. If you are on a fixed fee with these clients then that is profit gone. Not to mention the distraction factor and opportunity cost. Start by asking them to leave. Get rid of the bottom 20% of clients. Find clients who appreciate your work and you can make a profit on. Every firm has excess capacity (especially when they implement our workflow procedures) and that excess capacity should be used on attaining more clients. If you got rid of the 20% who are 'bottom feeders' and replaced them with new ones who were 'A' class then your profit would go through the roof.

According to the 6-year-old, profit is good and you should make as much as possible!

> Quotable quote:
>
> *"Every Accounting firm I have ever trained, coached or even spoken to has clients who are costing the firm money."*

Your services

Some services you offer are just not profitable. They are low-value services that attract a low-value price. Just like you measure 'average hourly rate' or 'net firm billing rate' on the business (at least I hope you are) why not start by doing that on every invoice and every service. It's a simple equation – invoice value/hours taken. You'll soon start to see which services have a low margin compared to others. Once you know the margin you can make a decision – keep or go. If you keep the service or product, then can it be done more efficiently by someone else somewhere else? Remember, you are not a community service. You do not have to do everything for everybody. Focus on services that have a ridiculously high margin and you'll improve your profit.

According to the 6-year-old, profit is good and you should make as much as possible!

Your clients buying more services

I am yet to meet an Accounting firm that has 'tapped out' every client with every service they have to offer. The objective is *'every client should be buying every service they need that helps them achieve their goals.'* That means you know the goals of the client and you are matching services to those goals. Time and time again I ask Accountants if their clients need additional services that you have the skills to deliver. I get the same answer every time. YES. The cool thing about additional services to existing clients is it is not more compliance work. It's more useful 'business advisory' and 'value added services' work. And the other cool thing is that these new services can be priced differently because the client has not bought it before and it has more value to the client. More value to the client = more margin for you = more profit.

> Quotable quote:
>
> *"Time and time again I ask Accountants if their clients need additional services that you have the skills to deliver. I get the same answer every time. YES."*

According to the 6-year-old, profit is good and you should make as much as possible!

Your leverage

Most firms are 'over partnered' and 'under leveraged.' This means that the ratio of people:partner is typically low. Many firms operate under the old practice model that they need about $1M in fees per partner and that means about 4-5 people in that team. What if

> Quotable quote:
>
> *"Yes. Fewer Partners and greater leverage = more profit per Partner."*

there were 15 or 20 people in the partner team? Or more. You'll get more leverage and your profit per partner will go through the roof. If you have low leverage then consider re-structuring your firm so the next 2 levels under the Partner must have more client contact, thus enabling the firm to have more clients per Partner and more revenue per Partner. There are too many overpaid Accountants who because of tenure and cash are currently Partners. They are not bringing in new business – merely looking after existing business. It's crazy to pay (with dividends) a Partner who adds a minimal growth value of $350k when you can hire a Senior Accountant for 1/3 of that and still get the same effect. Yes. Fewer Partners and greater leverage = more profit per Partner.

According to the 6-year-old, profit is good and you should make as much as possible!

Here is an example of all of that put together. This firm is a picture of good health. It is not a super profitable firm @ 48% before partner salaries (we have some firms >60%) yet it is a very solid firm with good client numbers, low risk and a modest average fee per client of $7,000 (project value of $1,750 x no. projects 4) and reasonable leverage of 7:1. In this firm the Partners are not doing a huge amount of client work (506 hours), nor is the Accounting team (1265 hours). The focus is not on 'more billable hours' but on value, and the output of value is the Average hourly rate (or Net Firm Billing rate) of $307. The firms that are using our **www.panalitix.com** programs and resource center, are the ones that are changing and making bigger profits.

KEY AREA	NOW
Partners	2
Accountants	10
Administration & Marketing	4
Client numbers - groups	600
Average client project value	$1,750
Number of client projects per year	4
Average fee per client group per year	$7,000
Revenue	$4,200,000
Salaries - excluding partners	$1,280,000 (30%)
Office overheads	$920,000
Total costs	$2,200,000
Profit before partner salaries	$2,000,000 (48%)
Profit per partner	$1,000,000
Productivity / Utilization - Partners	30% (506 hours)
Productivity / Utilization - Accountants	75% (1,265 hours)
Average hourly rate / Net firm billing rate - client hours	$307
Average hourly rate / Net firm billing rate - all hours	$155

What do you want your profit to be? If you are comfortable where you are at then ignore everything I have written. If you are looking for more then there is more available.

To Remain Relevant in the future you need to increase your profit. The 6-year-old kid thinks it's a good idea and so do I.

How to be super-efficient and still make money

When a partner of an Accounting firm says to a colleague or team member:

> *'I want more billable hours out of you' or 'I need you to get more time on the clock' or 'Your utilization/productivity is low – fix it.' What are they saying?*

They are basically saying that the individual is not performing. When in actual fact they may be. The individual that you are 'performance managing' may actually be super-efficient however the traditional business model says that they are not.

The traditional business model of an Accounting Practice (not a business) is to 'put time on the clock' for a client and then based on the hourly rate of the individual(s) doing the work this will determine the price. When you say you want more time on the clock from the person typically bad behavior starts to enter the equation. Team members go slower, they 'pad' time sheets out, they make mistakes, they go 'hunting' for issues, they double/triple check everything and basically spend more time then they need to.

Don't you think it's amazing that when you say to an Accountant *'you've got $5,000 worth of billable time on this job'* and just like magic the job comes in at around $5,000? You see, Accountants fill the available time with what work they have to do.

> Quotable quote:
>
> *"Accountants fill the available time with what work they have to do."*

Let me make it very clear: if you are pricing in arrears and driving more billable hours, then this is a very bad thing. You are not promoting efficiencies. You are promoting inefficiencies.

If you continue to price in arrears and you do decide to get efficient then what happens is the price either goes down with the new efficiencies or you end up doing more work for the same amount of money. Not a good look!

Being more efficient is the way to go however you MUST price the project upfront if you want to capitalize on the investment you have made in being more efficient.

The diagram below shows you the new profit model for a modern and progressive Accounting firm.

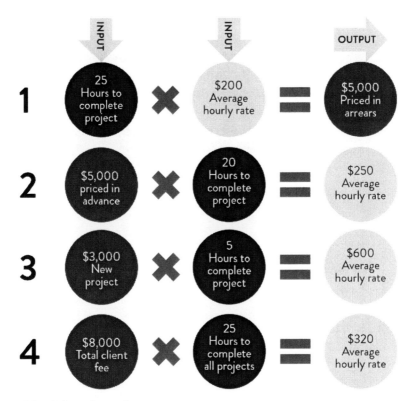

Here's how it works:

Step 1 is the old model. You put time on the job (input), you have charge rates (input) and the price pops out the end as an output. You are promoting inefficiencies and write-offs. Stop doing this immediately.

Step 2 is part 1 of the new model. You price upfront (sometimes for the same amount), you get as efficient as you can and take time out of the job (in this case 5 hours taken out) and the average hourly rate (in this case $250) pops out at the end.

Step 3 is part 2 of the new model. You 'value price' a new project (in this case $3,000) to the same client, you use the 'saved' hours (in this case 5) to deliver the new project and the average hourly rate (in this case $600) pops out at the end.

Step 4 is the outcome of 2 & 3. Your new fee to this client is $8,000, the time taken is still 25 hours and the average hourly rate is now $320.

Imagine if you did this across your entire firm? Imagine taking your average hourly rate (or net firm billing rate) from $200 to $320. What if your firm did 10,000 client hours? Your previous revenue was $2,000,000 and your new revenue for the same 10,000 client hours is $3,200,000. The difference ($1,200,000) is mostly profit. Are you excited yet?

> Quotable quote:
>
> *"Imagine taking your average hourly rate (or net firm billing rate) from $200 to $320."*

But how do you do this? How do you get efficient (I'll deal with pricing upfront and value pricing later) and take time out of every single client job?

> Quotable quote:
>
> *"I have observed that there are 8 key ways to get super-efficient with any Accounting or advisory project."*

After many years helping Accounting firms to be more efficient, I have observed that there are 8 key ways to get super-efficient with any Accounting or advisory project. The premise on this list is that you have a good team of people so I am not covering that here. Here is the list of 8:

1. Client Service Coordinators
2. Self-imposed deadlines
3. Policies & Rules
4. Visual management
5. Technology
6. All information in from clients
7. Getting rid of bottlenecks
8. Scheduling of work

Let's look at each one.

Client Service Coordinators

It's a known fact that Accountants spend a big chunk of their day doing administration work as part of every accounting job. Depending on the skill level of the team member the number of hours per person per day varies. Often the more skilled and senior the more administration they do. Typically the average is 1.5 hours of administration work (associated with the accounting task) per Accountant per day. If you have 10 Accountants that's 75 hours per week and if they work for 48 weeks of the year that's a whopping 3,600 hours spent per year doing administration work. If you have an average hourly rate (net firm billing rate) of $200 then that's equivalent to $720,000 of administration time (aka opportunity cost) per year. If you hired 2 new people (called a Client Service Coordinator or CSC) to look after the 10 Accountants and take the administration tasks off them then you'd free up $720,000 of capacity. Even if you filled 50% of the new capacity you'd still be a mile in front on what you pay the CSC's. The strategy is sound and it works. Send me an email and I'll send you a position description.

> Quotable quote:
>
> *"If you hired 2 new people (called a Client Service Coordinator or CSC) to look after the 10 Accountants and take the administration tasks off them then you'd free up $720,000 of capacity."*

Self-imposed deadlines

It always makes me laugh when I observe people who are about to go on vacation for a few weeks. Have you noticed that they are super-efficient in the final weeks leading up to the vacation? Their meetings are shorter, they talk faster, they type faster and emails are much shorter and to the point. Previously they used to give a long-winded answer and now they simply say 'NO' and hit send. Why? Because they had a self-imposed deadline and they didn't want to go away and still be thinking about work. The efficiencies are real when you have self-imposed deadlines on Accounting work. Here are some examples of self-imposed deadlines:

- You could tell the client when you'll be getting the work back to them – you could even book the presentation meeting
- You could have a maximum hours budget on every job
- You could impose a 10-day turnaround time on every job
- You could create an internal competition on time taken and accuracy

When you get a culture of self-imposed deadlines you build a culture of efficiency seeking.'

Policies & Rules

What rules or policies have you got regarding your workflow management process? You can have client policies and team policies. For example every project has a 'maximum hours budget' (not a dollar budget as the price has already been set) and that budget is always challenged down. You should always be asking the question 'how can we do this job in ½ the time?' You could collect

> Quotable quote:
>
> *"A non-negotiable rule is that every job is priced upfront and the client is notified of the scope of works and the price of the project."*

some money from clients before proceeding. A rule could be that you don't start the job before all of the client information/data has been collected. A policy should be not to go outside of the scope of works – only do what you're supposed to do and everything else is priced separately. A non-negotiable rule is that every job is priced upfront and the client is notified of the scope of works and the price of the project. If you're going to have rules then make sure you stick to them.

Visual management

Some Accountants like to hide behind screens and spreadsheets all day. Have you ever wondered what they actually do all day as they sit there quietly? It's very easy to hide behind 2 or 3 computer screens. It's not so easy to hide behind a big screen or whiteboard that shows their 'real time' performance. A visual management system is great for motivation, accountability and transparency. Below is a template of a very good one. The thing I like about this 'whiteboard' is that is has 3 self-imposed deadlines built in. The due date, the maximum hours and the 10-day turnaround commitment. Every day the job is in the shop, a day is added. Every day the board is updated with 'hours to go' based on the maximum hours budget. You can see which clients / jobs are on schedule and off schedule. The objective of this board is to get the work in and out in 10 days with a credit balance on the hours at the end. Once the job is finished a file note is created of how many hours it took and the margin on the job. That way you can beat it next year!

ACCOUNTANT	CLIENT/JOB	DUE DATE	MAX HRS	1	2	3	4	5	6	7	8	9	10	HRS TO GO
Mary	Coleman	3/2/15	24	24/1	25/1	26/1	27/1							12
	Dunn	4/2/15	16	26/1	27/1	28/1	29/1	30/1	31/1					5
	Pillans	5/2/15	28	26/1	27/1	28/1	29/1	30/1						28
John	Henson	31/1/15	9	28/1	29/1									0
	Vanjicki	15/2/15	15	3/2	4/2	5/2	6/2							1
	Fitzalan	12/2/15	21	6/2	7/2	8/2	9/2							12
Hamish	Ware	1/2/15	8	5/2	6/2	7/2	8/2	9/2	10/2	11/2	12/2			2
	Hillig	22/2/15	44	3/2	4/2	5/2	6/2	7/2	8/2	9/2	10/2	11/2	12/2	·6
	Mansell	16/2/15	22	26/1										18
Jane	Wilson	5/2/15	12	28/1	29/1	30/1	31/1	1/2	2/2					7
	Kelly	9/2/15	8	26/1	27/1	28/1	29/1	30/1	31/1	1/2	2/2			-4
	Challenger	11/2/15	9	26/1	27/1									9

Once you have the screen or whiteboard in place it's the perfect place to hold the daily stand up workflow meeting.

Technology

Many Accounting firms I visit and initially work with are operating with technology from 10+ years ago. They still have servers, paper management systems, single screens and their clients are on multiple versions of accounting software. Time to get with the program, folks. **The advent of 'cloud' technology is THE most significant efficiency gaining tool ever created for accounting firms.** No more version control issues, all documents are on the Internet, real time data from clients and supercomputers are doing the processing work. You need to actively and assertively get all of your clients onto a cloud accounting system. You need to convert your 'Practice Management System' to a cloud system and you need to get rid of the filing cabinets. When you get your clients on a cloud accounting system you can consolidate their data into software like **www.panalitix.com** (subtle plug again) and offer valuable business advisory services to them. **You and your clients' data accessed anytime, on any device and from any location.** What's not to like about that?

All information in from clients

I find Accountants have a nasty habit of not being very clear on what they want their clients to send in. I also find that clients have a nasty habit of not sending in everything when they are asked. I also find that Accountants are not that quick to follow up on the missing information.

> Quotable quote:
>
> *"All this missing information leads to 'job pick up put down' and massive inefficiencies. So fix it."*

All this missing information leads to 'job pick up put down' and massive inefficiencies. So fix it. All you need to do is get your new Client Service Coordinator to send a (plain English) questionnaire to the client with enough detail so we can locate what you need. Then have the CSC call the client to check that they got it, that they understand it and then make them accountable to a date when the client will have it all sent in. Give the client the deadline plus a day and then call them to see where it is. If they miss the new deadline then have the CSC physically go to their place of work and collect it. Do not let Accountants 'rip off an email' to the client asking for the information and then waiting. And waiting and waiting and waiting. Have the CSC manage the process.

Getting rid of bottlenecks

When you apply 'The theory of constraints' to a manufacturing line it'll be the slowest part/section/process/person that holds up the speed of throughput. A manufacturing line exists in an accounting firm and every accounting project. There is a process to follow,

> Quotable quote:
>
> *"Find out what the bottlenecks are and fix them. They are causing you to be inefficient."*

there is information to collect and a product needs to be created from the process and the information. Along the way there are 'bottlenecks' that are slowing up progress. There could be a bottleneck with clients, technology, certain team members and even the Partners. Find out what the bottlenecks are and fix them. They are causing you to be inefficient.

Scheduling of work

I visit accounting firms and I see piles and piles of folders and paper. It's like a visual filing system is going on. There are low rise piles and high rise piles. Sometimes the piles fall over they are so high and unstable. Sound familiar. There can only be one logical reason that there are so many jobs in the shop at any one time. There is no scheduling of when it is supposed to come in. Clients are just sending in their 'stuff' when it suits them. If I go to a Dentist I have to book in as the Dentist can only see one person at a time. Speaking of Dentists. I visited an accounting firm once and I asked them how many open jobs they had at that moment in time. Tap tap tap into their workflow system and it showed 440 open jobs. They had 20 Accountants so that was 22 open jobs per accountant. I was at a dinner party a couple of nights later and I meet the Dentist. In casual conversation I told the Dentist about my visit and 22 open jobs for each Accountant. The Dentist replied '*that's like me having 3 patients in 3 separate chairs at any one time. I'd make mistakes. No wonder they're inefficient.*' Schedule the known work (when you're doing it and when you need it) at least 6 months in advance and make sure each Accountant has no more than 3 open jobs at any one time.

The pursuit of efficiency is what you must do to thrive in this profession. You'll need to stop driving billable hours and if you price every job upfront, refill the newfound capacity with business advisory services so you'll make a lot of money and you'll have very happy clients.

Old pricing models are unethical

I am using the 'ethics' card right upfront to get your attention. I personally feel that pricing by the hour in arrears is an unethical way to price. Here's why:

When you price by the hour you are not incentivized to be as efficient as possible and get the job done super-fast. In fact, you are directly incentivized to do the task slower. You are incentivized to over analyze and take your time. You are incentivized to 'pad out time sheets' and in some cases make mistakes.

And it gets worse when management (aka Partners) actively promotes and measures 'productivity,' 'utilization' and 'billable hours' targets. I'll give you 6.5 hours a day charged to the client says the eager Accountant who wants to impress. I'll go a little slower and I'll do things in the job that I didn't need to do. I'll even leave the clock running as I go to the bathroom. I'll start the clock as I am driving to the clients' office. I'll keep it running as we have lunch together. And seeing we charge in 6 minute 'units' then if a task takes 45 minutes I'll just round it up and charge 8 units. With all that (the eager Accountant says) I got my daily target.

Is there anything more unethical than that? At this point in time you may think of sending me some hate mail. That's OK; you're entitled to your opinion. My contact details are in the front and the back of the book!

Seriously, though. Pricing by the hour for professional services has got issues written all over it.

Other than what I have mentioned earlier here are some more examples:

> Quotable quote:
>
> *"At this point in time you may think of sending me some hate mail. That's OK; you're entitled to your opinion. My contact details are in the front and the back of the book!"*

- ➤ How can a relationship be enhanced when the client is worrying about 'when does the clock start' when they meet with you?
- ➤ The price per hour assumes that the salary level of the person is correct.
- ➤ The project assumes the time taken was correct?
- ➤ Why would you invest in super-efficient processes and technology – your price will drop.
- ➤ You give the Accountant $5,000 'worth of time' to do the task and miraculously they take $5,000 worth of time. That's after they have gone faster, gone slower and stopped the clock a few times.
- ➤ You will always (always) get write downs when you price by the hour in arrears.

And lastly, what about the poor client? They have no idea what the bill will be until it arrives.

I understand that nearly every other Accounting firm in the world does it this way. I understand that's the way it's been done for centuries. It doesn't mean it is right. I think since the introduction of the computer on everyone's desk in the 1990's the issue has been exacerbated. The introduction of the 'background time sheet' and 'electronic time sheet' has fueled the unethical fire.

> Quotable quote:
>
> *"I think since the intro-duction of the computer on everyone's desk in the 1990's the issue has been exacerbated."*

I think there is only one option forward. That is to tell the client the price and scope of every single project in advance and in writing. The client signs off on the price and scope and you get to work and do the job as efficiently as possible. That's it. Nothing more, nothing less.

Now you can get creative with this and give your clients an enhanced version.

You could package up a number of services (known ones) and give your client an 'Annual Accounting Service' which is an annual fee divided by 12 to get a monthly fee. Then have a direct debit authority for the monthly fee.

You could promote known services into 'packages' on your website. It's the old 'small, medium and large' idea.

BASIC	INTERMEDIATE	ADVANCED
Cloud accounting software	Cloud accounting software	Cloud accounting software
Lodgment of quarterly BAS/Tax/GST	Lodgment of quarterly tax	Lodgment of quarterly tax
Lodgment of annual return	Lodgment of annual return	Lodgment of annual return
Year end review meeting	Year end review meeting	Year end review meeting
Unlimited phone and email support	Unlimited phone and email support	Unlimited phone and email support
Regular tax updates	Regular tax updates	Regular tax updates
	Interim financial statements	Interim financial statements
	Year end tax planning	Year end tax planning
		Annual cashflow forecast
		Monthly cashflow report
$250 *Per Month*	**$450** *Per Month*	**$750** *Per Month*

Note: This is a guideline only and not designed to be the price to charge or the package to promote. Also, I am sure you could come up with more creative titles then I have here.

Or you could simply scope out every project and offer a written price to your client before you start.

I am reminded of an old marketing saying '*it is arrogant in the extreme to dictate to the marketplace how much they will pay and what they will buy.*'

> **Quotable quote:**
>
> *"It is arrogant in the extreme to dictate to the marketplace how much they will pay and what they will buy."*

What that means is you come up with an idea/price/package and you 'put it out there' and see how the marketplace responds. If they buy it too easily then play with the pricing until you get some saying no. If they consistently ask for 'this but not that' then play with your packaging. Let the marketplace tell you what they will buy and how much they will pay by testing.

Your clients deserve a price before the project starts. You deserve to be rewarded based on being as efficient as you can. Your team needs to be incentivized for going fast rather than slow. And lastly, you also need to be rewarded for the value you create for your clients not the time it took to do the task.

Pricing on value

The problem (here I go again) with pricing by the hour is that the assumption is that the price per hour is correct (often calculated by a salary multiple) and the time to do the task was correct. The assumption is that time multiplied by the rate equals the correct price. In my view, nothing could be further from the truth.

When selling intellectual property to price in arrears based on time and rate is a bizarre pricing model. You are valuing what you know and the outcome the client gets based on a salary multiple (to get to the charge rate) and the time taken to do the task. Very strange! I understand it's an easy way to calculate a price. The issue is this model does not value how smart you are and the impact you make.

There has to be a better way. And there is. It's all about value pricing. Value pricing is where you price the job

> **Quotable quote:**
>
> *"Value pricing is where you price the job upfront based on the value you create for your client."*

upfront based on the value you create for your client. You cannot value price after the fact. That means you have to 'scope' the project out first (by talking with the client and doing some research), find the value you are adding and then present an implementation plan to the client based on how you are going to help them.

Now for historical work you have a challenge with pricing. And that's price parity. You may think it is worth more but if the client has been paying $X for the past few years then they may pay $X + a bit – but not the price you think it is worth. For a new project that the client has not bought before then that's a different story.

If you know the numbers in advance (cloud accounting helps with that enormously) then you can scope out projects that make a difference with your clients. If you can articulate your value in advance and present it in such a way that makes sense financially and emotionally then you'll win the business.

> Quotable quote:
>
> *"If you can articulate your value in advance and present it in such a way that makes sense financially and emotionally then you'll win the business."*

Most people get the concept of value pricing. Price based on your value.

The biggest question I get around this topic is '*how do I work out the price?*' Here is the definitive way to price knowledge-based services. If you follow this simple guide you'll never need to ask the question again.

There are only 3 areas you need to focus on to get to the right price.

1. Your value belief in the project, your team and yourself
2. You value contribution to the client's condition
3. Your client's value perception of what you are doing for them.

The diagram below will help you determine the right price.

GETTING TO THE IDEAL PRICE

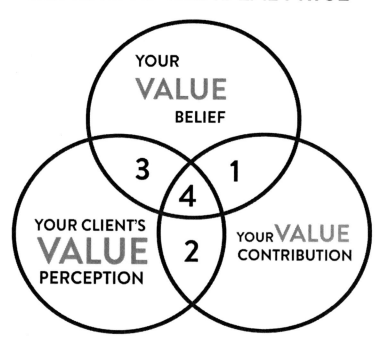

Here are some pricing scenarios around these 3 critical pricing areas.

Let's say you have a high value belief and your contribution is high (zone 1) yet you have not articulated your value to your client then you will not maximize your price. Let's say your client value contribution is high and your client's perception of your value is high (zone 2) yet your self-belief is low then you will not maximize your price. The worst one is when your client's value perception is high and your value belief is high (zone 3) yet your contribution is low then you will not maximize your price – you're basically lying!

If you want to maximize your price and get a great return on your intellectual property then all 3 areas must be working together. You need to be in zone 4.

Let's look at each one in detail and see if I can help you with the dark art of pricing.

Your value belief

It all starts here. Unless you believe in yourself and what you and your firm know is worthy of a high price then you will always price low. I find self-esteem in the Accounting profession to be a major issue when it comes to pricing. You might be different but most of those who I meet lack the confidence and courage to price appropriately.

> Quotable quote:
>
> *"Unless you believe in yourself and what you and your firm know is worthy of a high price then you will always price low."*

As you look at the scope of work to do and as you work out the value you'll scratch your head (like the Accountant below) and you'll have a lot of 'chatter' going on in your head. You'll be thinking of charge rates, value, competitors and the one you most think of is *'what will my client think?'*

LIMITING PRICING BELIEFS

Who cares what others think?

Get over yourself. They are not really thinking about you. They too busy worrying what you think of them! What people think of you is none of your business anyway, that's their business.

Get some courage and believe in your self-worth as an awesome, smart Accountant. It's taken you years to get to where you are today. You used to do the same project in 5 days now because of your experience you can do the same project in 2 hours. You should be rewarded for your years of experience, and not how long it took to do the project.

> Quotable quote:
>
> *"You should be rewarded for your years of experience, and not how long it took to do the project."*

Here's your new value belief system:

> *"I really value what I know. I articulate my value eloquently. I sell my intellect and information based on my value contribution rather than my time"*

Your value contribution

To work out your value contribution you are adding you need to think about the following:

Without me, they can achieve 'X' result. With me they can achieve 'Z' result. The difference ('Y') is your value that you can add. The impact might be financial, emotional or both.

Let's look at a couple of examples.

Cash-flow improvement. If the client is constantly juggling cash, never has any surplus money and always stretching creditors and arranging payment plans then that is the current situation. If you can educate them, put systems in place, show them how to improve profit and then monitor their behavior, and let's say the outcome over the year is that they are $200,000 better off. Your cash 'value add' is $200,000. They are also sleeping better at night, less stressed, have more working capital to expand and are generally happier. Your emotional value add is massive. How much would you charge? Well a 10:1 return is a pretty good deal. So maybe $20k - $30k.

Tax minimization. If your client has a tax exposure of say $550,000 because of their current structure and trading environment then that is the current reality. You come along and re-structure their affairs and negotiate with the tax department and you get their exposure down to $150,000. Then your cash value add is $400,000. What can they do with $400,000? Maybe expand the business, pay the family home off sooner, retire early and get some of their life back. Your emotional value add is huge. What's that worth to the client? Pick a number – maybe $30k - $60k.

Without high value contribution you will not maximize your price. You need to work it (value contribution) out in advance and show the client with confidence that you can help them.

> Quotable quote:
>
> *"Without high value contribution you will not maximize your price."*

Your client's value perception

How you articulate how you are helping your client improve their condition will make a massive difference in whether a) you win the business in the first place and b) you maximize your price.

It's all in the language. And if you want to master the dark art of pricing then you need to become an eloquent user of value pricing language.

Here's the problem that must be addressed.

Most Accountants talk to their clients about what they are going to do rather than what they are currently doing will do for the client.

What I mean is most Accountants talk to me about inputs (activities) rather than outputs (results). Most Accountants tell me all of the work they have to do rather than what benefit I will get when I buy the work.

I see engagement letters that look like this:

Included in this project is:

> Quotable quote:
>
> *"Most Accountants talk to their clients about what they are going to do rather than what they are currently doing will do for the client."*

➢ Analysis of your current situation
➢ Recommendations to improve your structure

➢ A cashflow forecast statement
➢ Tax planning for entities X, Y & Z
➢ Annual financial returns for entities X, Y & Z
➢ Personal financial returns

Throw in an audit and you have the entire shopping list at the grocery store!

INPUTS OR OUTPUTS

✗ Analysis	✓ Profit
✗ Advice	✓ Growth
✗ Budgets	✓ Cashflow
✗ Tax planning	✓ Security
✗ EOY statements	✓ Wealth
✗ Meetings	✓ Retirement
✗ Valuations	✓ Success
✗ Consulting	✓ Peace of Mind
✗ Structuring	✓ Lifestyle
✗ Time	✓ Hope

You must change your language and articulate the BENEFITS of the project. It's the oldest radio station in the world W.I.I.F.M – What's in it for me!

Talk to me about profit improvement, wealth creation, asset security, life style improvement, etc. Just tell me how much better off I'll be by buying your ideas.

At the end of the day the only right price is what the market is prepared to pay for it. That means the right price is just before NO. In other words if they keep saying YES without hesitation then the price is too low.

Value pricing is a wonderful tool to use. It gives certainty to the client of the price and the scope and you maximize the years and years of experience you have.

Chapter 10
It's all about you

In Chapter 2 I wrote about 'Business by Design' and I mentioned that you should design your business by your rules and the way you want it to be. You're taking all the risk so you should have all the spoils. Many Partners of Accounting firms get the concept and they agree with the theory. What I find is that they often lack the personal development to pull it off.

I have been fortunate to have been involved in the 'Personal Development' space since 1987 – two years after I left school at age 16. I have attended hundreds of seminars, read hundreds more books, listened to hundreds of hours of audio, viewed hundreds of hours of video and devoured countless manuals, websites, articles and papers on a quest to become a better me.

I have always believed that if you want to run a better business then you must become a better business person. I also believe that the development of the business will never outpace the development of its leader.

> Quotable quote:
> *"I have always believed that if you want to run a better business then you must become a better business person."*

So to round out the last chapter of this book I am going to focus on 12 critical traits for becoming a better you. They are 12 traits that when implemented fully will serve you well on your quest to become the best business leader you can be.

Here's how this chapter works. I will explain the critical area and you are to score between 1 & 10 how you are on each of the critical areas. The scoring guide is below.

On each trait on my 'Spider Wheel' put a mark where you fit. In the middle is 0 and the outer point is 10.

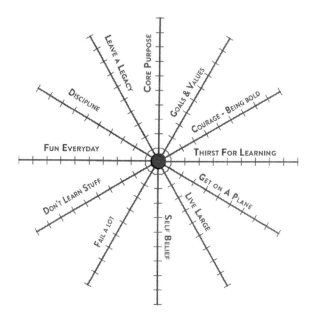

I've got 12 key traits to cover. Do not score on the spider wheel until you have read the trait. Of course, the more honest you are with yourself the more success you'll have.

Your core purpose

Why do you do what you do every day? What is your reason for being on this Earth for this very short amount of time? Some people call this your 'WHY' and others your core purpose or your mission in life.

I found my core purpose in 2006 in Bali, Indonesia. I was attending an Entrepreneurs conference and I was asked to sit down with one of the speakers and do an 'exercise.' We'd just finished playing golf and he (Thomas) ordered from the barman 20 pieces of paper and 1 beer each. Thomas said at the end of it I would have my core purpose and I would cry like a baby. For the next 3 hours Thomas asked me question after question about me and at the end 2 words popped out.

"Influencing Lives"

Not changing lives but influencing lives. This is what I am all about. I like to influence. I like to make a difference. I can't change someone's life but I can influence it. I like to write, speak and develop products and services that influence. I like to get the feedback on how people have used my ideas and concepts. I love case studies and success stories. One of my core values in business is to influence lives. We align business decisions to our values. As a business we want to make sure that we are influencing lives every day.

Thomas was right. I did cry like a baby when I discovered my core purpose in life. What's yours?

If you know your core purpose and you live by it then score yourself a 10. If not, score what you feel is right for you.

Your goals and values

There have been countless studies done on the fact that if you write down your goals then you have a good chance of achieving them. Most people plan their holidays better than they plan their lives.

There is a lot of talk about goal setting but very little on the process of achieving the goals. So I thought I would give you in detail **my goal achievement process.**

Let me just start by saying that I have been setting and achieving goals for over 30 years. My first major goal achieved was to be the Under 15 Australian Archery Champion. I achieved the gold medal in 1984. Then I had a goal to be the Under 18 Australian Archery Champion. I achieved that one in 1987. It was the same year I 'got into' personal and business development material.

Over the years I have fine-tuned my goal setting and goal achievement into a process which works for me. Here it is...

1. I **handwrite** everything into a very special annual journal. I buy it from the UK luxury stationer, Smythson of Bond Street, London. I have the journal customized with my name and the current year.

2. At the back of the journal I have all my **life goals listed** – currently 171 of them. I update this every year before the start of the new year.

3. In the journal I also have my **personal values**, my over-arching **purpose in life**, my constant **energy and focus state, what's important to me** and a list of my **beliefs** – all handwritten.

4. Throughout the year I will collect as many pictures as I can (from magazines) of my life goals and put them onto my **vision board.** I will also have a visual management process so I can see how I am doing in achieving these goals.

5. I write at the front of my journal a **list of goals for this year.** There are typically 20 listed for each year – however 5 are the most important. The top 5 are highlighted. Most of the goals for the year are from my full list – either moving towards achieving them or completing them.

6. Once all goals are listed I reflect back on the last year and work out why I did not achieve all of my stated goals. Something has to be done differently. I write down what I am going to **start doing** differently, **stop doing** and **continue doing.** Each one covers a page in the journal.

7. For goals that take time to achieve **I block out time in my diary for the entire year for each one.** I block out... family day trips, board meetings (monthly), accountability meetings (monthly) management meetings (weekly), seminars to attend (typically 12 -16 days per year), known seminars to deliver, gym sessions (3 per week), bike riding (2-3 per week), blog writing (2-3 per week), date nights (monthly), dinner parties we will host, holidays (8-10 weeks), golf lessons (many), golf practice (not enough), golf playing (1-2 per week – not enough), me weeks, camping trips, school holidays, etc. Everything is blocked out and then I work with what is left. It's amazing how much time is actually left for random stuff or extra work if needed when the year is blocked out. I have a view that **if it's not in the diary it won't get done.**

8. I write down **action plans** for each of the goals on my annual list. So fun, business, personal, health, family, relationship, etc. Bullet point action plans for the ones that need it.

9. **I only divulge my goal list to people who are going to help me get them.** It's private. So that includes my wife, my accountability group and some goals for my management team and employees.

10. **I keep myself accountable** to my goals each month by my accountability forum.

11. **I review and read my goals** every week.

12. Whilst achieving my goals I live by all of my core values especially **finishing what I start and doing what I say I am going to do.**

To make all this happen I still sleep 7-8 hours per night and I wake up at 0445 6 days per week. I want to milk everything out of this life and be the best I can be. I love living up to my core purpose and having great stories to tell of my experiences. As I said this works for me – it may even work for you.

My personal values are interwoven into my goals. I want to make sure that I am living my short life in line with my values, whilst checking off my goals in life.

If you have your goals written down and you have a process for achieving them then score yourself a 10 on the spider wheel. If you have no written goals (typed or handwritten) then that's a '0' score for you!

Courage and being bold

I find the fear of failure stops a lot of people. There is an acronym for FEAR. False Evidence Appearing Real. It does take courage to do something different. The lack of courage causes the dreaded P word – procrastination. As the late Zig Ziglar used to say with considerable gusto – 'Procrastination is the assassination of motivation.' I always look at the issue/challenge/target or whatever it is as 'what's the worst that can happen?' If it's only losing a bit of money as the worst that can happen then I'll typically give the go ahead. If the data stacks up and we believe in our abilities then we do it. Sometimes we win, often we fail. But at least we had a go.

> Quotable quote:
> "As the late Zig Ziglar used to say with considerable gusto – 'Procrastination is the assassination of motivation.'"

The challenge the Accounting profession has is it is too comfortable. The business of Accounting is changing, however it's still a comfortable business to be in. Here's my view of what being comfortable does to a business...

Comfort breeds apathy
Apathy breeds procrastination
Procrastination breeds lack of innovation
Lack of innovation breeds stagnation
Stagnation breeds death!

To succeed in business I think the leadership needs a healthy discontent with the present.

I have had the privilege of meeting one of this world's great Entrepreneurs, Sir Richard Branson, a few times. He is known for his business acumen and his 'just do it' attitude to life. However as I discovered on a number of occasions he does not jump into projects or businesses without research, data and careful consideration. He told me once that they always 'protect the downside' when they start a business or get involved in one. As he described to me 'if the planes go down the trains can't.' He has the courage to try different things and push the boundaries but he does it with a calculated view.

How are your courage levels? If they are outstanding give yourself a 10. If not then mark a score that reflects your current courage and boldness for trying new things.

Thirst for learning

How curious are you? How many questions do you ask? How many 'non-technical' books/webinars/audio/video sessions do you read/participate in/attend? How often do you read your national financial newspaper? How many business visits do you go on to learn how you can do it better?

These are questions that indicate your ongoing thirst for learning. I meet a lot of Accountants who only do the required 40 hours of CPE/D per year. Typically these events are technical related which is great if you want to be a better Accountant. What about being a better person? What about being a better business person? What about being a better communicator/leader/mentor/marketer?

I think there is too much time spent on 'technical' learning then what might be called 'soft skills.' It's the soft skills that define us. It's the soft skills that will propel us forward. I am fortunate to associate with many high profile entrepreneurs and leaders. The thing they all have in common is their thirst for learning. They tend to have a systematic learning program of reading, viewing and attending.

> Quotable quote:
> *"I think there is too much time spent on 'technical' learning then what might be called 'soft skills.' It's the soft skills that define us."*

This book is about Accountants and one characteristic I find bizarre is how Accountants do not ask that many questions. I often wonder if asking a question is seen as a weakness with Accountants. I think the opposite. I think asking questions is a sign of curiosity, interest and intelligence. I know some people are naturally shy and reserved. Maybe

that's the problem – not enough confidence and low self-esteem.
What is going to be your annual learning plan?

- ✓ Number of books to read
- ✓ Number of courses to attend – locally and internationally
- ✓ New skills to learn
- ✓ Businesses to visit

Maybe you need to hire a mentor or a coach. Whatever you decide, make sure you are learning something new. If you're not learning you're not growing. If you're not growing don't expect your business to grow beyond the development of you.

If you are outstanding at this give yourself a 10 on the rating scale. If not maybe there is something in this trait you can work on.

Jump on a plane

I have the view that someone somewhere has done what I want to do. They could be in another city, state or even another country. Wherever they are I want to find them. And I do find them. Often that means jumping on a plane to go meet with them. I will respect their time and I will listen intently. The biggest compliment I can give is to implement what they told me and then write them a thank you note with what I have done.

Most people I meet are not prepared to jump on a plan. They complain about the cost, the time and the hassle. Yes, quality air travel in a good seat near the front of the plane can be costly! However the benefits outweigh the costs. The person / company you are about to meet might be a world leader in your field. They may have some insights that could save you years of work and millions of dollars in mistakes.

I am a keen golfer and often random people say to me 'can I give you a tip?' My standard answer is NO. Unless you are a teaching professional who has runs on the board I am not going to listen to

> Quotable quote:
>
> *"The person or company you seek may not be within driving distance of where you live. Sometimes you need to jump on a plane to seek them out."*

you. I want to learn and follow someone who has done it before. Not a '15 handicapper' who has read some magazines!

The person or company you seek may not be within driving distance of where you live. Sometimes you need to jump on a plane to seek them out.

Living large

My personal success mantra is 'doing what I want, when I want, with whom I want in a manner I want. The last point (manner I want) is all about me living my life the way I want to live it. That means I like to live large!

Life is for enjoying and there are many things that make life that little bit

more enjoyable. I like to fly business or first class on every flight. I like to sleep in 5-star hotels. I like a driver to pick me up wherever I travel to. I like good clothes / food / wine. I like to drive quality cars. I like to donate money to charity. I like to have a cool office in the coolest street in town. I even like to go glamping, glamour camping! I have a camping wine rack among other cool camping gadgets. That's an example of the manner in which I like to live.

When it comes to Accountants living large, they may desire to live better but they have a big concern. The concern is *what will my clients think?* Many Accountants have moved offices and had the customary office opening party. A client will make a smart remark that your fees are likely to go up now. Or you'll buy a new car and a client will comment that they now know why their bills are so high.

The vast majority of clients will not say anything yet most will remember the client that made the smart comment. I think of it this way. What someone thinks of me is their business and it's none of my business – it's their business.

Why not be proud of the fact that you are successful. I think people in the advisory space should be more successful than those they advise.

I came back from Las Vegas once after buying 3 pairs of really cool cowboy boots. I wore them out one night to a client function. One of my clients quipped '*oh, that's where our fees are going.*' I said YES, and thank you!

If you are living the life you want to live then score yourself a 10. If you are too afraid of your clients, mark a 1. It's not about flaunting it. It's about being proud of what you have achieved.

Bucket loads of self-belief

My favorite Maori (New Zealand indigenous people) word is 'MANA' pronounced 'Marrrna' – according to the online Maori dictionary it means:

(noun) prestige, authority, control, power, influence, status, spiritual power, charisma – mana is a supernatural force in a person, place or object.

I love this word. That person over there has Mana. When they walk in the room they have presence, they command the room and they are in control. When they speak they speak with authority and charisma. They are influential in everything they do.

Do you have Mana? Who do you know has Mana? I think Mana is what self-belief and self-esteem is all about. To succeed in business you need Mana. You need to have self-belief and a high self-esteem problem.

I have a view that there are too many Partners of Accounting firms in the Accounting profession. Many Partners are there for retention reasons not good business reasons. I meet many Partners who are overpaid Client Managers just doing the job they did before they became a Partner. They have not stepped out of their comfort zone; they are not creating new business and new opportunities. Even when they try to create some new business they are unsuccessful compared to others.

> Quotable quote:
>
> "*I meet many Partners who are overpaid Client Managers just doing the job they did before they became a Partner.*"

They are not doing this because they do not have the personal development, self-belief, and confidence to be a super-success.

Most don't have much Mana!

Here are my top 10 tips for increasing your Mana. Geez, I love that word!

1. **People you hang around with.** If you want to be successful hang around with successful people. It will rub off. It's not about hanging around with the 'loud' people. Sometimes people who are overly talkative and loud are masking their own self-esteem.
2. **Material you absorb.** What content are you reading/watching/ listening to? There is a rich source of self-development material for free on the Internet or if you're like me, you buy copious amounts of books and attend seminars regularly.
3. **Client successes.** Take a look at what you have done for your clients in the past. What have you helped them with? How have you made them successful? Realize that without you they wouldn't be what they are. You are amazing!
4. **Team successes.** How have you helped your team grow and develop? How are they better off since joining your firm? Take the successful stories and relish in them!
5. **The way you dress.** The old saying '*the clothes maketh the man*' is very true. How do you dress? You don't have to be in $2,000 suits but a wardrobe makeover can make a world of difference.
6. **Looking at your accomplishments.** Your career is littered with great successes. From awards, to certificates to stories, letters and testimonials. How often do you reflect on what you have done? Be proud of yourself on what you have accomplished to date.
7. **Be happy in your own skin.** The health and fitness industry is booming by telling people they are fat, unfit and about to die if they don't do something about themselves – TODAY. Ok, if you are obese and a health risk then do something about it. But why not be happy just the way you are and live life well now?
8. **Goals and affirmations.** I have 4 pages on written beliefs, affir- mations and energy state every day. I read it constantly to keep myself 'up.'
9. **Positive exterior.** Do you carry a smile on your face or a scowl? When someone asks you how you are, how do you reply? Not bad. Pretty good or OK – all negatives. Why not reply with great, booming, enjoying myself or something more positive. And sometimes you have to fake it until you make it.
10. **Self-talk.** This is the big one. What do you say to yourself when

there is no one around? Is the chatter so negative that it stymies your development? Does it make you fearful of the world? STOP IT.

Self-belief is such a critical key to success. It's not about being arrogant just being sure of yourself. It's time to get some more Mana. Wimps need not apply!

Go ahead and score based on where you believe you are now versus where you want to be.

Fail a lot

If you're not failing you're not growing! Who knows where I got that from but it is true. To fail means you are 'having a go' and you are trying new things. I have tried so many things/ideas/processes/ strategies/business models and I must say most have not worked. A few good ones work really well.

> Quotable quote:
>
> *"If you're not failing you're not growing! Who knows where I got that from but it is true."*

But I keep trying and never give up. I keep reading & learning and implementing. I have a healthy discontent for the present which means I am always looking for the next idea. This drives my team crazy sometimes but they're used to it by now.

One of my most 'epic fails' of my business career was a few years ago when I had this idea that I could leverage my very successful coaching business around the world. I was looking for a 100 licensees who could coach Accountants in a geographical area. Those coaches would each have 100 Accountants as clients and in turn each Accountant would have 100 small business clients signed up to our online software platform. We called it 100^3. It was a flawless plan on the spreadsheet and the slide deck. It was a $100M business opportunity (on paper) waiting to happen. We marketed the program and got 650 enquiries from around the world in a matter of weeks. We only needed 12 to validate and get going. We built a team to support it and spent a fortune on IT platforms as well.

How could we fail? Well, it did.

The reason it failed was because we were looking for the perfect type of person. Someone who could hit the ground running with minimal training. If we lowered our standards then we could have found hundreds (as many franchise coaching companies have) who could potentially do the role. We weren't prepared to do that. Instead we canceled the program and moved on.

As a small business at the time (circa $5M in revenue) it ended up costing $1.5M. With no borrowings in the business that came out of cashflow. Ouch, ouch and more ouch! We licked our wounds for a couple of years on that one. We had a go.

We failed and we learned. Out of the exercise, we ended up with an awesome IT platform (**www.panalitix.com**) that is now used by thousands of Accountants around the world.

So from failure there is sometimes a silver lining.

I find Accountants do not fail enough because they do not do enough. They are too comfortable doing what they are doing. Maybe if technology (software and robots – not kidding here BTW) replaced Accountants in the future you would be more active in trying new ideas.

> Quotable quote:
>
> *"Maybe if technology (software and robots – not kidding here BTW) replaced Accountants in the future you would be more active in trying new ideas."*

Where are you at on my annoying rating scale? If you are trying a lot and failing a lot (as long as you learn) then rate it a 10. Otherwise score it lower.

Don't learn stuff

In the year 2000 I relocated my family from Sydney to Brisbane. When I met the furniture removalist I asked him if he had a lawnmower. The answer was no. I said you do now and I gave him mine. I have never mown a lawn since. Nor do I intend to. I choose to do tasks I like doing and that I am good at. If I like

> Quotable quote:
>
> *"I choose to do tasks I like doing and that I am good at. If I like doing a task I learn how to use the tool to do the task."*

doing a task I learn how to use the tool to do the task. If you look at office equipment there are many tools that make life easier that I don't want to learn how to use.

Take the scanner. It's a useful tool but I'm not going to learn how to use it. If I do I may have to use it. Or what about that thing with sharp teeth called the binding machine? That thing can hurt you. There are trained professionals who know how to use the binding machine. I don't want to be one of them.

I like to get focused on the '*3 highest dollar productive activities*' that I can do in my business life. I am brutal with my time on this and I don't do what is not a 'top 3' activity or I delegate it to someone else.

In the year 2005 I started my Accountants coaching business from home. Within a couple of weeks of my new startup I wrote in permanent ink on my white board the following:

I will only do 3 things in this business:
1. *Marketing*
2. *Selling*
3. *Delivery*
I will only not work for anything less than $750 per hour.

Remember this was 2005. My self-esteem was not as high as it now and that's why I priced my time at $750 per hour. Pretty quickly I took that to $1,000 then $2,000 then $3,000 then I moved to value based fees and it didn't matter anymore.

These days my top 3 have changed. My business has grown and I have a team of people around me who are professionals in what they do and I am a professional in 3 things only.

1. **Leveraged marketing.** Writing this book is a good example.
2. **Strategic thinking.** Basically coming up with ideas
3. **Leadership.** Inspiring the team to greatness

I currently still do a little bit of direct client work (around 10% of my time) but over time that will cease. If I can spend 80% of my time on my top 3 then the business is better off for it and so am I.

This chapter is all about you. You are the primary risk-taker in your life and you should get the spoils. Go ahead and rate yourself where you are about learning 'stuff' versus what you would like not to know!

> Quotable quote:
>
> *"If I can spend 80% of my time on my top 3 then the business is better off for it and so am I."*

Fun everyday

In 2001 I started my first software business. It was all exciting at the start (as all startups typically are) and super busy. We raised quite a lot of cash to get it going and we were away. As the co-founder one of my roles was sales. I was selling every day to my target market. It was tough work but the product was working, the clients liked it and we were making a difference. However I was not enjoying it. In 2005 we decided we should chase some big fish and that meant looking for distribution in the USA. I went for a visit, met with the key people in the target company and they also liked what we had. It was all going great and they verbally said they wanted to distribute the product throughout the USA. I was excited.

A few weeks after returning home I had a 0430 phone call with the key people in Chicago. I got a *'not now'* answer from them. It turned out to be a big fat '**NO.**' At 0445 I put my head in my hands and I actually beat my head against my desk. Why is this so hard? Why is this not working for me? Why am I not enjoying it? The day prior to this call (October

> Quotable quote:
>
> *"I had received my test results of my 'Wealth Profile' – which path I should follow to create wealth and enjoyment in business."*

25, 2005) I had received my test results of my 'Wealth Profile' – which path I should follow to create wealth and enjoyment in business.

I looked at the test results and I instantly realized I was in the wrong business – for me. I could not be 'me' in the business and I felt the business was boring. Something had to change. I waited until 0730 and I called my then business partner. I said I needed to see him. He asked what it was all about. I said I'll tell you when I see you. A couple of hours later I was at his home and I told him that I was not enjoying it and I wanted to leave. He said when. Today was my answer. He said you can't leave today and he also said, what are you going to do? I said I didn't know what I was going to do but I am going to follow this 'Star' thing and see where it takes me. My mind was made up and I ended up leaving 2 weeks later. They gave me a nice send off and I was out of there.

I had no money, no method of making money, no assets, kids in private schools, car leases and a mortgage. I had the whole thing going on. That weekend I was at a friend's house at a BBQ and he too asked me, what am I going to do? I had no idea. He gave me 3 ideas which I followed through on. One of them (coachingclub) turned out to be a $30M (and counting) idea.

So I started a new business from home. The first month I did $2,000 in revenue. The 2nd month $22,000. The 3rd month $24,000 and by the time the first 12 months finished I did $975K in revenue. I made a profit of $450k in my first year and in the 2nd year over $1M in profit and have never looked back. Since that day (October 26, 2005) when I decided to take massive action I have been in my flame (not in the wax) and enjoying business and having fun literally every day.

The business of business should not be a drag. If you have designed it your way then surely that involves having fun and enjoying the journey.

How much fun are you having? Are you passionate about what you are doing? If it is 'off the charts' fun every day then score a 10. If it is a drag and it's not working and you're not passionate about it then score lower. And do something about it. It's a business and we're only here once!

> Quotable quote:
>
> *"The business of business should not be a drag. If you have designed it your way then surely that involves having fun and enjoying the journey."*

Having the discipline to succeed

All top performers have immense discipline. The top performing person could be an Athlete, a Musician, a Politician, a Spiritual leader, a Salesperson a Doctor or a Business owner. It doesn't matter what field the person is in, the successful ones all have a disciplined approach to success.

So how does discipline make its way into an Accounting firm? Here are 7 examples that require discipline.

1. Workflow processes. Do you have a process? If you do is it followed every time? I bet not. My guess is sometimes you do it, sometimes you don't. We created an 18 step workflow process which works with every Accounting job no matter what source of software you use. Every Accountant we teach it to loves it and when they implement it they get amazing results of efficiency, customer service and margin improvement. One of the steps is to do a 'Business Performance Review' once per year using our **www.panalitix.com** software. Every single Accountant agrees it is the right thing to do and they agree they should do it at least once per year with every business client. Do they? Not likely. It takes discipline to follow a workflow process.

2. Meeting rhythm. We endorse (originally learned from Verne Harnish) and teach regular stand up meetings which are designed for quick communication. Every Accountant we teach it to loves the idea. They're supposed to start at an odd time (0909, 1010) and go for a short amount of time. There are 3 questions asked of each team member 1) What's up? 2) What's your daily metric? and 3) Where are you stuck? The ones that follow it get amazing results of communication and problem solving. Do they always follow it? Not a chance.

> Quotable quote:
>
> *"Every Accountant we teach it to loves the idea. They're supposed to start at an odd time (0909, 1010) and go for a short amount of time."*

3. Systematic growth. If you want to double the revenue of your firm in 3 years then you need 26% revenue growth per annum or 2% per month. Month in month out. If you want to double in 5 years then you need 15% per annum growth or 1.2% growth per month. Month in month out. To grow a business you need a systematic approach to marketing, sales and service. Each month builds on the last month. It takes discipline and focus.

> "To grow a business you need a systematic approach to marketing, sales and service. Each month builds on the last month. It takes discipline and focus."

4. **Sales meetings.** I strongly endorse that Partners should do a minimum of 20 client visits per month with existing clients. The objective to see where the client is at with their business, understand their objectives and then see if they need any help (new services) to achieve their objectives. Let's call it what it is. It's a sales meeting. They take about 90 minutes per meeting and then with some follow up (write a document and maybe meet again) it might take another 90 minutes. So 3 hours per client X 20 clients = 60 hours per month. If you did this (and you were really bad at sales) then you'd get at least 5 new projects per month. The ones who have been trained in our sales methods are getting 15 projects from 20 clients. Let's be conservative and work on 5 projects per month from 20 clients. If each project has a value of say $7,500 (based on value based fees) that's $37,500 of new business. That's a $625 per hour return. It's a pretty good use of time and the client is better off for it. It takes discipline to do 20 meetings per month. Most don't but all should.

5. **Meeting times.** I like to schedule meeting times at odd times during the day. I'll call you at 1015. Let's meet at 0808. How about we catch up for coffee at 0940 on Tuesday? Then I like to play games with time. I like to watch the second hand on the clock get to the 12 and then start calling. I have exactly 60 seconds to connect with the person and most people look at the clock on their computer or their phone. I am calling precisely as agreed. I am meeting with you precisely as agreed. We are starting the meeting at precisely the time we agreed and we are not going over time in any way shape or form. I like to call out and I rarely let anyone call me. I do that because I know I will be on time with my meeting / calling schedule. It takes discipline to do this. Most people are sloppy with meeting times and many will say 'we'll get started as soon as such and such is here.' Not on my watch. I am not going to punish

those that are on time because a few people are late. Incompetent people are late. Competent people are sometimes behind schedule.

6. One thing at a time. I think 'multi-tasking' is a crock. How can you do 3 things at once really well? The human attention span is dropping every decade as our lives are flooded with more and more content and data every day. It's coming from all angles all the time. To

> Quotable quote:
>
> *"I think 'multi-tasking' is a crock. How can you do 3 things at once really well?"*

deal with all that life and business throws at us, the answer is not getting good at multi-tasking. The answer is to get focused on the one thing you have to do right now. Do it properly and once only. Do one project at a time only. Have one uninterrupted conversation at a time. Deal with emails when you deal with them – not emails, Facebook, phone calls and Twitter all at the same time. Have one open client job at a time and stay focused until it is done. If you attempt multi-tasking you'll enter into 'job pick up put down' syndrome which leads to inefficiencies and mistakes.

7. Saying no. If you know who your target market is and what services you offer then you need to stay true to that and say NO to potential clients, services and projects. If you have a business plan (I can send you an awesome sample one page business plan if you email me) and you set the objectives, priorities and projects at the start of the year then make sure you stick to them. Say NO to shiny

> Quotable quote:
>
> *"Say NO to shiny new things that may look good but may divert your course. It takes discipline to say NO more than YES."*

new things that may look good but may divert your course. It takes discipline to say NO more than YES.

At the end of the day it's about being true to your values, doing what you say you're going to do and finishing what you start. If you start something then take it through to the finish line. Sometimes you might not finish exactly in the timeframe you intended but at least you finished.

You know you better than anyone so score yourself really honestly on this one.

Leaving a legacy

When you're gone from this Earth what will they say about you? What are you building or doing that is making a difference? Have you written your own eulogy?

As the saying goes – we're only here for a very short time, not a long time. My life coach is an ex-Monk and he introduced me to my 'death' clock. I thought death was a bit harsh so I renamed it to my 'time to die' clock. It counts down every second on my smartphone and it is quite sobering to realize that I don't have much time left.

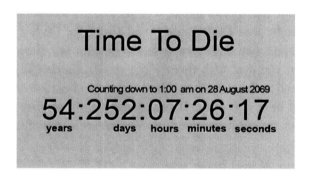

I set my clock at exactly 100 years old. I am going to checkout on (or thereabouts) on August 28 2069. I figured that 100 years is long enough.

In that time I want to live by my core purpose, have goals and values, be courageous, learn a lot, get on planes, live large, improve my self-belief, fail many times, don't learn stuff I don't need to, have fun every day, be super disciplined and leave a legacy!

For the last time, score where you sit on the Leave a Legacy scale.

So how did you do on your scores? Like most people you'll have some high and some low. It's time to join the dots. When you join the dots does it look something like this?

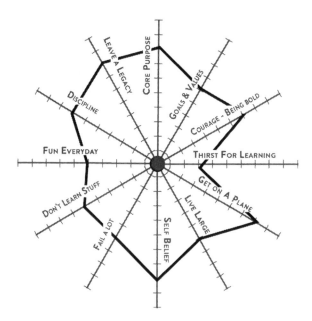

It is what it is.

The 12 traits are all about making a wheel. This is the wheel that will get you from A to B in your business life. This is the wheel that will keep you sharp as you strive to Remain Relevant.

What does your wheel look like? How is your wheel going to roll? Wheels are supposed to be round, aren't they? If you have a small round wheel (all 2's and 3's) then your journey to Remaining Relevant will be tiresome with a lot of effort and you'll feel every bump in the road.

If you have a large round wheel (all 7's and 8's) then the journey will take effort and you'll cruise over the bumps.

How do you want your wheel to look? Maybe it's time to pump up the tires!

The final word

Thank you for reading my book. I hope you enjoyed it. Now what? Are you going to just read it and then file it (aka do nothing) with the rest of the books you have read? Or are you going to take some action and implement the relevant ideas?

I learned this simple formula a long time ago...**Decisions + Action = Results**. If you liked what you have read then from here it's all about making decisions and then implementing them. You are only going to make some decisions and take some action if the result you seek is strong enough. What is that result for you and your firm? Is it revenue, profit, cashflow, wealth, happiness or client delight? Or maybe it's everything.

If you're just looking for a few tweaks here and there then you've probably wasted your time reading the book. Give the book to a colleague. Assuming you liked the book here are some action points:

1. Buy a copy for your team members
2. Connect with me on social media platforms (details below)
3. Subscribe to and read my blog (details below)
4. Send me an email with what free stuff you would like (mentioned throughout the book)
5. Sign up for a free Revenue, Profit and Capacity consultation (go to **www.panalitix.com**)
6. Create a list of all the possible projects you could implement
7. Implement 2-5 projects off the list every month
8. Let me know of your progress – what's working and what's not

If you're looking to Remain Relevant as a firm then maybe it's time to step up and make some significant changes. I have held nothing back in the book and provided a lot of my best content with significant details so you can implement it.

It's my hope that I have provided a good business case where you are influenced enough to take action.

All the best with your success!

Rob Nixon
January 2015, Brisbane, Australia

Contact details:
Email - rob@robnixon.com or rob.nixon@panalitix.com
Website - www.panalitix.com
Blog - www.robnixon.com
Twitter - @therobnixon
LinkedIn – therobnixon
Facebook - rob.nixon.969

Lightning Source UK Ltd.
Milton Keynes UK
UKOW02f0148190516

274557UK00004B/193/P